Cozy Cables

INSPIRED KNITTING
PATTERNS TO WARM THE
BODY AND SOUL

Kalurah Hudson
Creator of While They Play Designs

PAGE STREET
PUBLISHING CO.

PAGE STREET
PUBLISHING CO.

First published in 2022 by

Page Street Publishing Co.

27 Congress Street, Suite 1511

Salem, MA 01970

www.pagestreetpublishing.com

Distributed by Macmillan, sales in Canada by The Canadian Manda Group.

26   25   24   23   22   1   2   3   4   5

ISBN-13: 978-1-64567-679-9

ISBN-10: 1-64567-679-X

Library of Congress Control Number: 2022939291

Cover and book design by Kylie Alexander for Page Street Publishing Co.

Photography by Kalurah Hudson

Printed and bound in the United States

FOR CHARLOTTE,
WITHOUT WHOM THIS BOOK NEVER
COULD HAVE BECOME A REALITY.

Contents

INTRODUCTION 6

TIPS & TRICKS FOR CABLE SUCCESS 8

Quick Cables 14

PROJECTS TO KNIT FOR INSTANT
GRATIFICATION. BASIC CABLE STITCHES
USING BULKY YARN.

Bräcken Frost Hat 17

Cross Country Hooded Infinity Cowl 21

Snowbird Blanket Shawl 27

Snow Fern Cardigan 32

Portable Cables 56

FOR GRAB-AND-GO KNITTING.
SMALL-SCALE PROJECTS WITH
EASY-TO-MEMORIZE CABLE PATTERNS.

Smokestack Ankle Socks 59

Snowberry Hat 65

Snow Tracks Headband 71

Ice Chalet Cowl 74

Gifting Cables 80

PATTERNS FOR THOSE NEAR AND DEAR.
MORE THOUGHTFUL STITCH PATTERNS
AND INTRICATE CABLES.

Campfire Stories Hat 83

Campfire Stories Fingerless Mitts 93

Aspens Asymmetric Shawl 108

River Rock Throw 123

Self-Care Cables 130

SOMETHING SPECIAL FOR THE NUMBER
ONE KNITTER IN YOUR LIFE: YOU.
ENGAGING YET MEDITATIVE STITCH
PATTERNS TO HELP YOU UNWIND.

Winter Dreamer Pullover 133

Storm Flurry Wrap 139

Kindling Stockings 149

Cloud Cover Hood 155

ABBREVIATIONS 164

TECHNIQUES 165

RESOURCES 172

ACKNOWLEDGMENTS 172

ABOUT THE AUTHOR 173

INDEX 174

INTRODUCTION

Cozy Cables is the culmination of the past decade-plus that I have spent designing knitwear patterns. From the very beginning of my knitting journey, the driving force behind wanting to learn this incredible craft was cables. As I looked around me, whether it was in films or magazines or out on the street, I noticed beautiful cable-knit patterns that jumped off the wearer and directly into my field of view. I could not look away. And so, my fascination with cables began.

Unlike many other knitters and crocheters, I did not have this craft bestowed upon me by a dear mother or grandmother. That being said, I was lucky to have two parents who nurtured my creativity, just as they were creatives in their own right. It first began with watching my mother sew clothes for my siblings and me, and eventually I began helping her at her sewing machine, cutting the fragile pattern pieces that would go on to become beautiful garments for our family.

My mother wasn't the only maker in my childhood home. Growing up, our house was filled with hand-made furniture, oil paintings hanging on the walls of every room and always something yummy cooking on the stove, courtesy of my father. The son of a Japanese immigrant, he inherited the gift of cooking traditional meals from his mother, Yukiko. He is also a self-taught oil painter and woodworker. I will always treasure memories of helping my father in his workshop, with the sound of his old 8-tracks and the smell of sawdust hanging in the air.

Coming from such creative roots, I found myself dabbling in watercolor, photography, card-making, furniture restoration and a little bit of hand-quilting. But it wasn't until I began semi-weekly visits to my husband's parents' house for dinner that I really started on my path to becoming a crochet and knitwear designer. It was there that I began to study the beautiful, crocheted afghans that adorned my mother-in-law's couch. The intricate wraps of the woolen stitches mesmerized me. It was something so different from any sewn garment, oil on canvas or piece of furniture that I had seen before.

Soon, my sweet mother-in-law, Charlotte, sat me down in her living room and we reviewed the stitches together. As I stared down at them with her, I examined her face as she reflected on a specific time when this object was made. Her face and that moment are two things I will always cherish. It ignited the spark in me to make something special for those I love too. And that spark would eventually grow into a flame.

I am so appreciative of her for teaching me to crochet with patience, love and care. But I became even more so when she was later diagnosed with Alzheimer's disease. As the disease progressed, she would still pull out that afghan from the linen closet and sit me down to go over the stitches. Even though her mind was failing her, this art of making was still inside her. It had not left her. I would see that same face again. Watching her reflect on memories that still resided inside her. Those moments were not lost for her, they lived on. And they will live on inside me.

Sadly, we lost Charlotte to the disease in the spring of 2020. I know that without her igniting that spark, my journey likely would have stopped there. Without having those magical moments with her as she taught me how to crochet, I don't know that I would have had the same passion and drive to pursue the next stop along my journey, which was knitting. Without her, I probably would not have pushed myself to learn more new skills and eventually build a small business for myself from scratch, later designing and self-publishing knit and crochet patterns. So, for all of that, I have her to thank.

As the years progressed and as my small children grew, I still had that nagging urge to keep exploring and learning new things. And then it hit me, I could re-create those stunning cable-knit designs that had been living rent free inside my head for so long.

As I think back to the time when I first learned how to knit, those images of cable knitwear were a huge driving force. I had already learned how to crochet and had a few designs under my belt. But something was missing. There was more out there, just beyond the horizon. It was cables. And learning how to knit was the vehicle that would take me there. I suppose, in a roundabout way, you could say that the only reason I sought out knitting was so I could learn how to create cables. That may sound like a bold statement but it's true. So, thanks to numerous YouTube® videos and the help of a friendly co-worker, I ventured down the knitting path. Destination: cables. The rest, as they say, is history. Or rather, where we begin this book.

Wherever you happen to be in your own knitting journey, this book will supply you with cable patterns ranging from easy to complex. They're sprinkled throughout the book, which is organized by project rather than by cable difficulty.

This book is a collection of sixteen brand-new cable-knit designs, specifically curated for the cozy moments in your life. I hope that you'll be able to create special moments that turn into memories you can share with someone dear to you—just as Charlotte did for me. Those moments seemed to always happen in the winter, just when cozy designs were the most appreciated. Because of that, this collection is winter-inspired, though the patterns can, of course, be knit up during any time of year. I hope you fall in love with these designs and enjoy knitting them for all the special people in your life.

Kalurah Hudson

TIPS & TRICKS FOR CABLE SUCCESS

In this chapter, we'll start out with some of my best tips and tricks for knitting cables, helping you make all the patterns in this book with confidence!

IMPORTANCE OF FIBER

When starting out with cable patterns, you may find it easier to work with a smoother fiber—one that glides effortlessly across your needles, and on and off your cable needle. The last thing you want is to have to fight with your yarn as you try to create a cable. And speaking of fighting, try to avoid busy colorways and darker, more saturated tones. These will make cabling even more difficult when you're learning the technique, because they will make your stitches harder to see. Try to keep the process as simple and easy to see as possible.

NEEDLE MATERIAL

When it comes to your knitting needles, you may want to avoid a super slippery material, such as metal or plastic. I've found that knitting needles made from natural materials like bamboo or hardwood have a nice, warm feel that works well with a more slippery fiber.

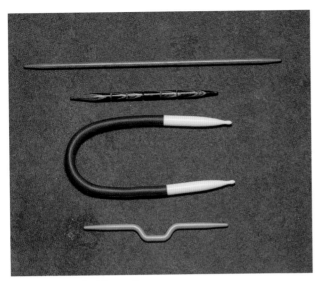

Various types of cable needles

CHOOSING A CABLE NEEDLE

As for the cable needle, there are a lot to choose from and making the choice can feel overwhelming. There are simple, straight ones, bendy ones and ones with unique shapes. I've found that cable needles that feature cool and kitschy elements like grooves in the middle or bendable rubber can just create issues instead of being helpful tools. For instance, your stitches can get caught on those grooves and snag your yarn. And while the flexibility of a rubberized cable needle can aid with keeping your stitches from falling off, your stitches can also stick to the rubber and be a bear to transfer off the needle when the time comes. These may not sound like huge issues but when you add them all up in a larger cabled project, you can lose a lot of valuable knitting time fighting with your cable needle.

So, when it comes to cable needles, I suggest you keep it simple. Look for one made from a smooth wood or plastic that has a simple U-shape in the middle. The little dip in the middle will ensure that your stitches stay on the cable needle. Also, look for a cable needle that has nice, tapered points on each end. This will make for an easy and quick transfer of stitches. And if you find yourself sans cable needle and have your set of double-pointed needles or interchangeable needle tips, either one makes a great cable needle in a pinch!

PRACTICE MAKES PERFECT

When practicing cables, if you stick to small projects such as washrags or a headband, you'll find the stitches less overwhelming to learn. Begin with a small number of stitches and try out cables with fewer stitches in them before moving on to larger, more intricate cables. Once you're comfortable moving onto a larger project, begin by swatching to get acquainted with the cable stitches in that particular pattern. Swatches themselves make for perfect practice.

HELPFUL TOOLS

You may find it helpful to have some locking stitch markers on standby to mark the placement of your cables. These can be easily removed and repositioned when your cable is completed.

Speaking of locking stitch markers, these are also great guides to mark the cabling rows in your work. For instance, a pattern may tell you to work five rows between each cable row. It can be difficult to read your knitting, so a locking stitch marker is a great visual reminder of where your last cable row was placed.

When following a pattern, you may also find it helpful to have a highlighter ready for marking your cable rows. Different colors can aid in keeping busy, intricate cable patterns straight. You can use a different color for different cables. This works well for both written and charted instructions.

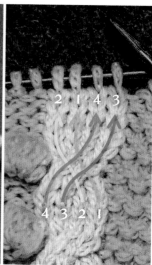

READING YOUR KNITTING

As I mentioned above, you may find it helpful to use a locking stitch marker to mark your cable row. But there's also a way to simply look at your knitting and see exactly where you've cabled, so you'll know how many rows to work before you cable again. (See photo above.)

As you can see in the photo, the stitches that were knit on the cable row all appear in a straight line. But the stitches directly below this row are distorted. So, when trying to locate the row you last cabled on, look for the first straight line of stitches. That's the cable row. From there, you can count each subsequent row of knitting that followed that row. This is incredibly helpful when you don't want to pay constant attention to which row you're currently working.

DROPPING YOUR STITCHES (ON PURPOSE!)

To better understand why on earth we would want to drop any of our stitches, let's break down the construction of a cable.

When you're making cables, essentially you're just reorienting the stitches on the left-hand needle before you work them.

In the photo, you can see that for a right-leaning cable, you want the third and fourth stitches to appear before the first and second stitches on the needle. Reorienting them on the needle (from right to left) as 3, 4, 1, 2 and then knitting them in their new order will create a right-leaning cable.

Slipping the first two stitches onto a cable needle and holding it to the back, for a right-leaning cable.

(1) Insert the right-hand needle into the third and fourth stitches purlwise, from right to left.

(2) Remove all four stitches from the left-hand needle.

Slipping the first two stitches onto a cable needle and holding it to the front, for a left-leaning cable.

(3) Quickly scoop up the first two stitches with the left-hand needle.

(4) All four stitches are knit in their new order.

Normally, this is where the cable needle comes in. For a right-leaning cable, it allows you to slip the first two stitches off your working needle and place them on reserve, in this case holding them to the back of your work. You can then knit the third and fourth stitches and slip the first and second stitches off the cable needle and onto the working needle and knit them in their new order. The right-leaning cable is complete. (See top photo.)

When working the left-leaning cable, you will also slip the first two stitches off your working needle but you will hold them to the front of your work. You can then knit the third and fourth stitches and slip your first and second stitches off the cable needle and onto the working needle and knit them in their new order. The left-leaning cable is complete. (See bottom photo.)

Now that we've covered how a cable needle is used, let's take the cable needle out of this process completely. Don't panic! Take a deep, relaxing breath.

First, let's work the right-leaning cable. Instead of slipping those first two stitches onto a cable needle, simply drop them off your working needle. But before doing so, you first want to secure the third and fourth stitches onto your right-hand needle. Essentially, the working needle (or right-hand needle as it were) will be acting as a cable needle here.

(1) To do this, just insert the tip of your right-hand needle into the third and fourth stitches purlwise, from right to left. (2) You can then remove all four stitches from the left-hand needle and (3) quickly scoop up the first two stitches again with the left-hand needle. Now, place the two stitches from the right-hand needle back onto the left-hand needle. Your four stitches are now reoriented on the left-hand needle as 3, 4, 1, 2 and you can knit them in their new order. (4) The right-leaning cable is now complete.

(1) Inserting the right-hand needle into the third and fourth stitches, from the back.

(2) Remove all four stitches from the left-hand needle.

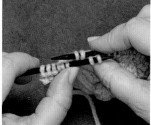

(3) Quickly scoop up the first two stitches with the left-hand needle.

(4) All four stitches are knit in their new order.

A locking stitch marker holds the reserved stitches.

As for working a left-leaning cable, you would do the same thing—almost. (1) When inserting the right-hand needle into the third and fourth stitches, you will do so from the back of your work. (2) You will then remove all four stitches from the left-hand needle and (3) quickly scoop up the first two stitches again with the left-hand needle. Place the two stitches from the right-hand needle back onto the left-hand needle. Now, you can knit the four stitches in their new order as 3, 4, 1, 2. (4) The left-leaning cable is now complete.

As you practice this technique, you may want to use a knitting needle with nice, tapered points. This will ensure easy gliding into the stitches that you'll be reorienting. You may also find it helpful to have a locking stitch marker handy to scoop up the dropped stitches. This can act as a security blanket until you get more comfortable with this method. (See photo above.)

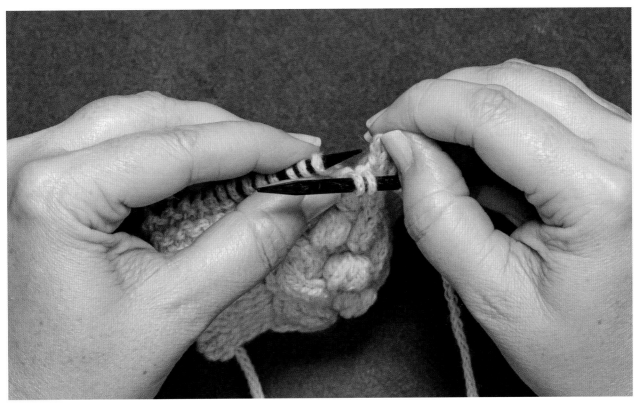

Use your fingers to reserve stitches when cabling without a cable needle.

Another tool that can help you keep those dropped stitches at bay is always with you—your fingers. Simply pinch the dropped stitches with your thumb and index finger when reorienting your cable stitches. It can be especially useful when working with a small number of stitches.

And speaking of the number of stitches, working sans–cable needle works best with fewer stitches. For cables that consist of eight or more stitches, it's much easier to use a cable needle.

Finally, my last tip for creating cables without a cable needle is to try and practice this method with sticky, grabby fibers. I know that I said earlier on that slippery fibers work best when cabling but when going

rogue, you want to use a yarn with grip. Use a yarn that will not immediately unravel when you drop the stitches. And the smoother the yarn, the more likely it will unravel. This isn't to say that you can't use slippery yarns, but starting out, you'll want to practice with a grabbier yarn.

I hope that you find these tips and tricks helpful as you practice cabling or continue in your cabling adventures.

As you work your way through this book, I just have a quick note regarding pattern difficulty. The difficulty levels listed in this book fall in line with the standards set by the Craft Yarn Council®. If you have questions regarding the difficulty levels, please see their website for more information.

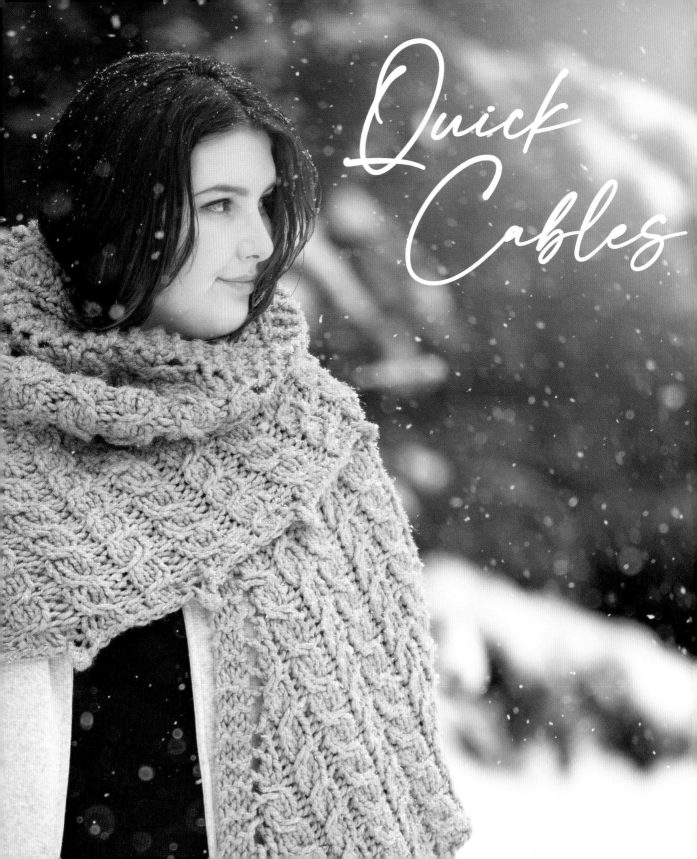

Quick
Cables

PROJECTS TO KNIT FOR INSTANT GRATIFICATION. BASIC CABLE STITCHES USING BULKY YARN.

This chapter will supply you with four patterns that you can reach for when you need a short and satisfying project to clear your busy mind. Bulky yarn is utilized here for quick knitting. Simple, straightforward cables will help you create a thoughtful, handmade object that won't bog you down. These projects also make great last-minute gifts when you're short on time.

I've included a hat, cowl, shawl and cardigan. You may be wondering what business a wearable piece like the Snow Fern Cardigan (page 32) has in this section. But with super bulky yarn, top-down construction and a progression of simple cables, this cardigan can be worked up in just one weekend! Best of all, there is no seaming required.

Bräcken Frost Hat

Bräcken is the Old Norse word for "fern." Resembling snow-dusted ferns that grow wild in the coniferous woodlands of the Pacific Coast in my home state of Washington, this trapper-style hat features a simple but gorgeous cable. An easy-to-memorize 10-stitch cable pattern is worked in super bulky yarn for instant satisfaction. Earflaps and long ties are added for additional warmth for long winter walks. The cable pattern works up fast and repeats itself every five rounds. This is the perfect project for travel-knitting or a cozy movie night by the fire. This pattern is charted and includes written instructions.

CONSTRUCTION

The Bräcken Frost Hat is worked in the round from the brim up. The earflaps are picked up from the cast-on stitches and worked in garter stitch. Long I-cords are worked for tying the hat securely beneath your chin. The pattern is written in one size that will fit a wide range of teen and adult heads.

Helpful tip: To maximize the yardage in your super bulky skein, when the hat is finished and before working the earflaps, weigh the yarn you have remaining. Cut that amount in half. Work your first earflap including the I-cord tie. You'll then have a better idea of how long you can work the I-cord tie for the second earflap.

SKILL LEVEL

Intermediate

SIZE

One size

FINISHED MEASUREMENTS

18 inches (46 cm) circumference and 9 inches (23 cm) height, blocked

MATERIALS

Yarn

Super bulky weight, Universal Yarn® Be Wool (60% acrylic, 40% wool), 94 yds (86 m) per 200-g skein

Yardage

90 yds (82 m)

Shown In

108 Platinum colorway (1 skein)

Any super bulky weight yarn can be used for this pattern.

Needles

For brim & body

US 17 (12 mm) 16-inch (40-cm) circular needle, or size needed to obtain gauge

For crown

US 17 (12 mm) DPNs, or size needed to obtain gauge

For earflaps

US 13 (9 mm) 16-inch (40-cm) circular needle, or three sizes down from needle you make gauge with

For I-cord

US 13 (9 mm) DPNs, or three sizes down from needle you make gauge with

(continued)

MATERIALS (CONTINUED)

Notions

- One 5-inch (12-cm) pom-pom (for hat)
- Two 3-inch (8-cm) pom-poms (for ties)
  - 2 cable needles
  - Stitch markers
  - Tapestry needle
  - Blocking materials

GAUGE

11 sts x 10 rnds = 4 inches (10 cm) in cable pattern in the round using larger needle (blocked)

SPECIAL TECHNIQUES

- Picking up and knitting stitches (page 170)
  - I-cord (page 167)

CABLE ABBREVIATIONS

All other abbreviations can be found on page 164.

- 2/2 RC = 2/2 right cable
- 2/2 LC = 2/2 left cable
- 2/1 RC = 2/1 right cable
- 2/1 LC = 2/1 left cable

SPECIAL STITCHES

- **2/2 RC:** Sl next 2 sts to CN and place at back of work, k2, then k2 from CN.
- **2/2 LC:** Sl next 2 sts to CN and place at front of work, k2, then k2 from CN.
- **2/1 RC:** Sl next st to CN and place at back of work, k2, then k1 from CN.
- **2/1 LC:** Sl next 2 sts to CN and place at front of work, k1, then k2 from CN.
- **CDD:** Worked over 3 sts. Insert RH needle through two sts from left to right knitwise, sl these sts off the needle, k1, then pass sl sts over the knit st. (3 sts decreased to 1).

Bräcken Frost Hat Pattern

HAT BRIM

With smaller needle, CO 50 sts using a longtail cast-on. Join in the round. Pm for BOR.

RND 1: (K1, P1) 25 times.

Work rnd 1 until your brim measures 2 inches (5 cm).

HAT BODY

Using larger needle, work rnds 1–15 of Bräcken Frost Hat Chart (page 20). Written instructions for the chart can be found on page 19.

HAT CROWN

Note: Switch to DPNs when needed.

RND 1: (K2tog, k6, ssk) 5 times. [40 sts]

RND 2: Knit.

RND 3: (Ssk, k4, k2tog) 5 times. [30 sts]

RND 4: (2/1 RC, 2/1 LC) 5 times.

RND 5: Knit.

RND 6: CDD 10 times. [10 sts]

Break yarn and weave tail through rem sts.

EARFLAPS

With RS of hat facing, turn the hat upside down so the cast-on edge is at the top.

Using smaller needle size, pu & k12 sts directly above one of the cable stitch repeats.

ROW 1 (WS): Knit.

ROW 2 (RS): K1, k2tog, k to the last 3 sts, ssk, k1. [10 sts]

ROW 3: Rep row 1.

ROW 4: Rep row 2. [8 sts]

ROW 5: Rep row 1.

ROW 6: Rep row 2. [6 sts]

ROW 7: Rep row 1.

ROW 8: Rep row 2. [4 sts]

ROW 9: Rep row 1.

ROW 10: K1, k2tog, k1. [3 sts]

I-CORD: Place the 3 rem sts onto a smaller size DPN, *slide the 3 sts to the right end of the needle and knit them again; rep from * until the I-cord measures approximately 12 inches (30 cm).

BO: K1, k2tog, pass first st over second st on needle. Break yarn and pull through rem st.

Repeat the second earflap on the other side of the hat, spacing them with a full cable chart repeat between the two. There should be one full cable repeat between the earflaps at the back of the hat and two full cable repeats between them at the front of the hat. See schematic.

FINISHING

Weave in all ends and block to finished dimensions. Sew the large pom-pom to the top of the hat and the smaller pom-poms to the end of the ties.

Bräcken Frost Hat Chart Instructions

RND 1: (P1, k8, p1) 5 times.

RND 2: Rep rnd 1.

RND 3: Rep rnd 1.

RND 4: (P1, 2/2 RC, 2/2 LC, p1) 5 times.

RND 5: Rep rnd 1.

RNDS 6–15: Rep rnds 1–5 twice. [10 rnds]

Bräcken Frost Hat Schematic

18 inches (46 cm)

9 inches (23 cm)

Bräcken Frost Hat Chart Key

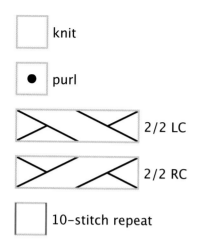

knit

● purl

⧄ 2/2 LC

⧄ 2/2 RC

10-stitch repeat

Bräcken Frost Hat Chart

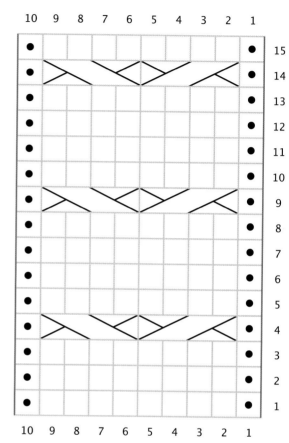

Cross Country Hooded Infinity Cowl

The Cross Country Hooded Infinity Cowl works up quickly on large needles using super bulky yarn. Like the long, gliding trails left behind by ski tracks, the big, bulky cables cross over each other as they work their way down the length of this cowl. A simple garter stitch acts as the backdrop for maximum squish factor. An oversized hood is added for extra coziness. Wear the cowl in one long loop or doubled up for extra warmth. This pattern is charted and includes written instructions.

CONSTRUCTION

This cowl is worked back and forth on straight needles and seamed together. The hood is made by picking up and knitting stitches using a long, circular needle and is seamed together at the top.

SKILL LEVEL

Intermediate

SIZE

One size

FINISHED MEASUREMENTS

Note: Because 100% wool is used, all measurements are taken unblocked.

Cowl

6½ inches (16.5 cm) wide x 68 inches (173 cm) circumference

Hood

12 x 12 inches (30 x 30 cm)

MATERIALS

Yarn

Super bulky weight, K+C Nordic Yarn (100% wool), 43 yds (40 m) per 100-g skein

Yardage

300 yds (274 m)

Shown In

White colorway (7 skeins)

Any super bulky weight yarn can be used for this pattern.

Needles

US 17 (12 mm) 32-inch (80-cm) circular needle, or size needed to obtain gauge

Notions

US 17 (12.75 mm) crochet hook

Cable needle

Tapestry needle

2 yds (2 m) of waste yarn in matching weight, for provisional cast-on

GAUGE

16 sts & 12 rows = 6½ x 4 inches (16.5 x 10 cm) per cable repeat, worked flat (unblocked)

SPECIAL TECHNIQUES

Provisional cast-on (page 170)

Picking up and knitting stitches (page 170)

Kitchener stitch (page 168)

Grafting in pattern (page 24)

CABLE ABBREVIATIONS

All other abbreviations can be found on page 164.

2/1 LC = 2/1 left cable

2/1 RC = 2/1 right cable

2/2 LC = 2/2 left cable

2/2 RC = 2/2 right cable

(continued)

SPECIAL STITCHES

- **2/1 LC:** Sl next 2 sts to CN and place at front of work, k1, then k2 from CN.
- **2/1 RC:** Sl next st to CN and place at back of work, k2, then k1 from CN.
- **2/2 LC:** Sl next 2 sts to CN and place at front of work, k2, then k2 from CN.
- **2/2 RC:** Sl next 2 sts to CN and place at back of work, k2, then k2 from CN.

Cross Country Hooded Infinity Cowl Pattern

PROVISIONAL CAST-ON
CO 16 sts using provisional cast-on. Leave a 20-inch (50-cm) tail for grafting.

Work rows 1–7 of Cross Country Chart (page 25) once. [7 rows]

Work rows 8–19 of Cross Country Chart 16 times. [192 rows]

Work rows 20–23 of Cross Country Chart once. [4 rows]

SEAM COWL
Remove provisional cast-on, placing live sts onto a second needle.

Fold piece together with the WS facing, meeting the top and bottom rows of sts. Break working yarn for weaving in later. Thread the CO tail onto the tapestry needle and follow the Grafting in Pattern instructions on page 24 to join the edges.

Break yarn when complete.

HOOD
Lay the scarf out with the RS facing you, horizontally, and locate the center of the scarf. This should be the area between two garter ridges. Count 10 garter ridges to the right of the center. Insert needle through the st at the top of the scarf, pu & k2 sts for each garter "ridge," picking up and knitting in this ridge and the next 19 ridges, ending 10 ridges to the left of the center. [40 sts picked up] Turn work.

ROW 1 (WS): Knit.

ROW 2 (RS): Knit.

Work rows 1–2 for 39 rows, ending on a WS row.

Distribute 20 sts onto one needle and 20 sts on the other.

Seam hood by folding the hood together with the WS facing.

Join using Kitchener stitch. Break yarn.

FINISHING
Weave in all ends. This pattern does not need to be blocked, so enjoy (or gift) your Cross Country Hooded Infinity Cowl immediately!

Cross Country Hooded Infinity Cowl Chart Instructions

ROW 1 (WS): K3, p2, k6, p2, k3.

ROW 2 (RS): K3, 2/1 LC, k4, 2/1 RC, k3.

ROW 3: K4, p2, k4, p2, k4.

ROW 4: K4, 2/2 LC, 2/2 RC, k4.

ROW 5: K6, p4, k6.

ROW 6: K6, 2/2 RC, k6.

ROW 7: Rep row 5.

(continued)

Grafting in Pattern for the Cross Country Hooded Infinity Cowl

STEP 1: Place both needles together, parallel to each other. Thread the tapestry needle knitwise through the first stitch on the front needle [a purl st] leaving the stitch on the knitting needle, then thread the needle through the first stitch on the back needle purlwise, leaving it on the needle.

STEP 2: Now thread the needle through the first stitch on the front needle purlwise and slip it off of the knitting needle, then thread knitwise through the next stitch on the front needle [another purl stitch] and leave it on the needle. Thread through the first stitch on the back needle knitwise and slip it off of the needle, then thread purlwise through the next stitch on the back needle and leave it on the needle.

Repeat Step 2 until your "next stitch" on the front needle is a knit stitch [stitch #4]. After slipping off the purl stitch before it [stitch #3], you will thread through purlwise. When it is this stitch's turn to be slipped off, you'll do it knitwise.

ROW 8: K4, 2/2 RC, 2/2 LC, k4.

ROW 9: Rep row 3.

ROW 10: K3, 2/1 RC, k4, 2/1 LC, k3.

ROW 11: Rep row 1.

ROW 12: Knit.

ROWS 13 – 18: Rep rows 1–6.

ROW 19: Rep row 5.

ROW 20: Rep row 8.

ROW 21: Rep row 3.

ROW 22: Rep row 10.

ROW 23: Rep row 1.

REMINDERS TO COMPLETE THE GRAFT

If the next 2 stitches on the front needle are knit stitches, slip the first stitch off the needle knitwise, then thread the needle through the 2nd stitch purlwise and leave on the needle. Do the opposite on the back needle.

If the next 2 stitches on the front needle are a knit, then a purl, slip the first stitch off the needle knitwise, then thread the needle through the 2nd stitch knitwise. Do the opposite on the back needle—slip first stitch off purlwise, thread through the 2nd stitch purlwise.

If the next 2 stitches on the front needle are purl stitches, slip the first stitch off the needle purlwise, then thread the needle through the 2nd stitch knitwise. Do the opposite on the back needle.

If the next 2 stitches on the front needle are a purl, then a knit, slip the first stitch off purlwise, then thread the needle through the 2nd stitch purlwise. Do the opposite on the back needle.

Cross Country Hooded Infinity Cowl Schematic

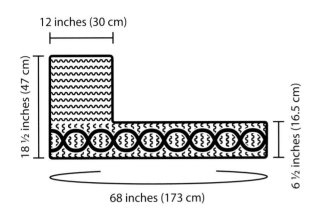

12 inches (30 cm)

18 ½ inches (47 cm)

6 ½ inches (16.5 cm)

68 inches (173 cm)

Cross Country Hooded Infinity Cowl Chart

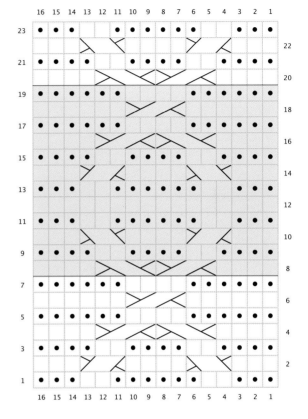

Cross Country Hooded Infinity Cowl Chart Key

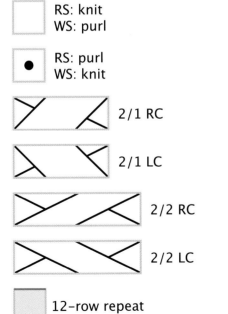

RS: knit
WS: purl

● RS: purl
WS: knit

2/1 RC

2/1 LC

2/2 RC

2/2 LC

12-row repeat

Snowbird Blanket Shawl

Forget flying south for the winter, warm yourself up with this fun and quick project instead. Snowbird is a simple triangle shawl that doubles as a wearable blanket. Like wrapping yourself up in a feathery down comforter, this blanket shawl features a very simple three-stitch cable that resembles distant birds in flight. With a four-row repeat, this is the perfect project for mindless knitting that will pay off with a finished shawl in just one day. A delicate picot edge helps balance out the chunky cables. This pattern is charted and includes written instructions.

CONSTRUCTION

This shawl is knit from the top down and is worked back and forth on long circular needles.

SKILL LEVEL

- Basic

SIZE

- One size

FINISHED MEASUREMENTS

- 30 x 70 inches (76 x 178 cm) wingspan, blocked

MATERIALS

Yarn

- Super bulky weight, Lion Brand Wool Ease® Thick & Quick® (80% acrylic, 20% wool), 106 yds (97 m) per 140-g skein

Yardage

- 500 yds (457 m)

Shown In

- Driftwood colorway (6 skeins)

Any super bulky weight yarn can be used for this pattern.

Needles

- US 17 (12 mm) 32-inch (80-cm) circular needle, or size needed to obtain gauge

Notions

- Cable needle
- 4 stitch markers
- Tapestry needle
- Blocking materials

GAUGE

- 16 sts & 24 rows = 6 inches (15 cm) in cable pattern worked flat (blocked)

SPECIAL TECHNIQUES

- Cable cast-on (page 165)
- Picots (page 170)

CABLE ABBREVIATIONS

All other abbreviations can be found on page 164.

- 1/2 LC = 1/2 left cable
- 1/2 RC = 1/2 right cable
- 1/1 RCU = 1/1 right cable unworked

SPECIAL STITCHES

- **1/2 LC:** Sl next st to CN and place at front of work, k2, then k1 from CN.
- **1/2 RC:** Sl next 2 sts to CN and place at back of work, k1, then k2 from CN.
- **1/1 RCU:** Sl 1 st to CN, place at back of work. Sl next st on LH needle purlwise onto RH needle, sl st from CN purlwise back onto the LH needle, place st from RH needle purlwise onto LH needle. (You have created a right twist without working the stitches.)

(continued)

Snowbird Blanket Shawl Pattern

GARTER TAB

CO 3 sts. Knit 7 rows. You will have 3 garter ridges in your work. Do not turn work.

(RS) Rotate work and pu & k1 st in each garter ridge along the edge of the piece [3 sts picked up], pu & k3 sts from the CO. [9 sts]

SET-UP ROW (RS): K3, pm, k1, pm, p1, pm, k1, pm, k3.

Note: The first and last stitch markers will separate the 3 garter sts at the beginning and ending of every row from the two chart repeats. The two middle stitch markers will separate the center spine stitch from the two chart repeats.

Work the shawl as follows:

RS ROWS: K3 (garter edge), sm, work chart, sm, k1 (center spine st), sm, work chart, sm, k3 (garter edge).

WS ROWS: K3 (garter edge), sm, work chart, sm, p1 (center spine st), sm, work chart, sm, k3 (garter edge).

Work Snowbird Blanket Chart A (page 30) once. [8 rows]

STITCH COUNT: 25 sts

Work Snowbird Blanket Chart B (page 31) a total of 5 times. [80 rows]

STITCH COUNT: 185 sts

BIND-OFF (RS): K1, place st back onto the LH needle, make picot.

(K1, place two sts from the RH needle onto the LH needle, k2togtbl) 6 times.

*1/1 RCU, place rem st from RH needle onto the LH needle, make picot, (k1, place 2 sts onto the LH needle, k2togtbl) 8 times; work from * 9 more times, (you'll be 5 sts from the center spine st).

1/1 RCU, place rem st from RH needle onto the LH needle, make picot.

(K1, place 2 sts onto the LH needle, k2togtbl) 6 times, place rem st from RH needle onto the LH needle, make picot, pu & k1 st from the center spine st, BO this st.

(K1, place 2 sts from the RH needle onto the LH needle, k2togtbl) 4 times.

*1/1 RCU, place rem st from RH needle onto the LH needle, make picot, (k1, place 2 sts onto the LH needle, k2togtbl) 8 times; work from * 9 more times, (8 sts rem on the LH needle).

1/1 RCU, place rem st from RH needle onto the LH needle, make picot.

(K1, place 2 sts onto the LH needle, k2togtbl) 7 times, (1 st rem on LH needle), place rem st from RH needle onto the LH needle, make picot, BO last st.

Break yarn and pull through rem loop.

FINISHING

Weave in all ends and block to finished dimensions.

Snowbird Blanket Shawl Chart A Instructions

ROW 1 (RS): Yo, p1, yo. [3 sts]

ROW 2 (WS): P1, k1, p1.

ROW 3: Yo, k1, p1, k1, yo. [5 sts]

ROW 4: P2, k1, p2.

ROW 5: Yo, k2, p1, k2, yo. [7 sts]

ROW 6: P3, k1, p3.

ROW 7: Yo, 1/2 RC, p1, 1/2 LC, yo. [9 sts]

ROW 8: (K1, p3) 2 times, k1. [25 sts]

Snowbird Blanket Shawl Chart B Instructions (Work 5 times)

ROW 1 (RS): Yo, p1, *k3, p1; rep from * to m, yo. [11 sts]

ROW 2 (WS): P1, *k1, p3; rep from * to 2 sts before m, k1, p1.

ROW 3: Yo, k1, p1, *1/2 RC, p1, 1/2 LC, p1; rep from * to 1 st before m, k1, yo. [13 sts]

ROW 4: P2, *k1, p3; rep from * to 3 sts before m, k1, p2.

ROW 5: Yo, k2, p1, *k3, p1; rep from * to 2 sts before m, k2, yo. [15 sts]

ROW 6: P3, *k1, p3; rep from * to m.

ROW 7: Yo, 1/2 LC, p1, *1/2 RC, p1, 1/2 LC, p1; rep from * to 3 sts before m, 1/2 RC, yo. [17 sts]

ROW 8: *K1, p3; rep from * to 1 st before m, k1.

ROW 9: Yo, p1, *k3, p1; rep from * to m, yo. [19 sts]

ROW 10: P1, *k1, p3; rep from * to 2 sts before m, k1, p1.

ROW 11: Yo, k1, p1, 1/2 LC, p1, *1/2 RC, p1, 1/2 LC, p1; rep from * to 5 sts before m, 1/2 RC, p1, k1, yo. [21 sts]

ROW 12: P2, k1, *p3, k1; rep from * to 2 sts before m, p2.

ROW 13: Yo, k2, p1, *k3, p1; rep from * to 2 sts before m, k2, yo. [23 sts]

ROW 14: P3, *k1, p3; rep from * to m.

ROW 15: Yo, *1/2 RC, p1, 1/2 LC, p1; rep from * to m, yo. [25 sts]

ROW 16: *K1, p3; rep from * to 1 st before m, k1.

STITCH COUNT AFTER 5 REPEATS: 185 sts

Snowbird Blanket Shawl Chart Key

	RS: knit WS: purl
●	RS: purl WS: knit
◯	yo
⧄	1/2 RC
⧅	1/2 LC
▨	no stitch
▨	8–stitch repeat

Snowbird Blanket Shawl Chart A

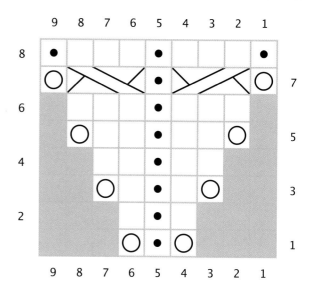

Snowbird Blanket Shawl Schematic

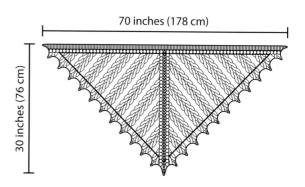

70 inches (178 cm)

30 inches (76 cm)

Snowbird Blanket Shawl Chart B

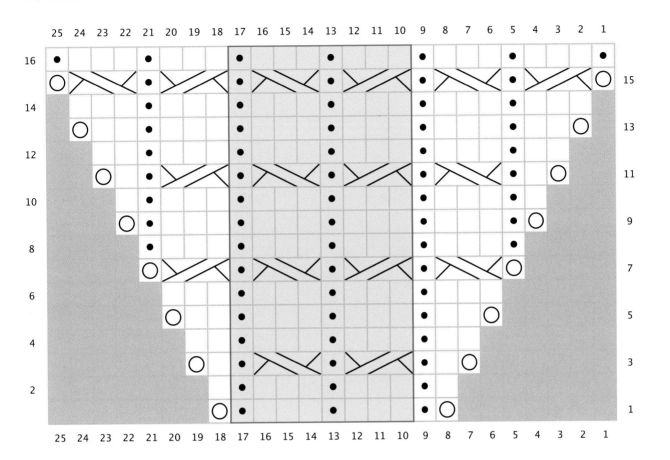

Snow Fern Cardigan

Snow Fern features unique cables that begin narrow and slowly expand out and back in again like the ferns that grow wild in the nearby Blue Mountains of Washington state. When the mountain snow covers the ground, these ferns resemble woolen stitches, which is what inspired this design. Snow Fern is a streamlined cardigan with narrow panels of cabling on the front and a wider panel of cables on the back. Raglan increases form the yoke of the cardigan. A faux seam runs down the sides for a polished look and a little extra structure. The sleeves are nice and roomy and feature bubble cuffs. This pattern is charted. For written instructions and downloadable charts, please visit https://whiletheyplaydesigns.com/SnowFernWrittendirections/ (password: cozycables).

CONSTRUCTION

This cardigan is worked back and forth from the neck down with raglan increases. The sleeves are separated, and the body is worked without any shaping. Stitches are picked up along the neck and front sides for the collar and front bands. The sleeves are knit in the round from the top down.

SKILL LEVEL

- Complex

SIZE

- 1 (2, 3, 4, 5, 6) (7, 8, 9, 10, 11, 12)

Finished bust

(This measurement includes both front ribbed bands) 35¾ (40, 44, 48¼, 51½, 55½) (59½, 63½, 67¾, 71¾, 75¾, 79¾) inches / 91 (101.5, 112, 122.5, 131, 141) (151, 161, 172, 182, 192.5, 202.5) cm, blocked

Recommended ease

This cardigan is designed to be worn with 6 to 8 inches (15 to 20 cm) of positive ease. Choose the closest size to your actual bust measurement plus the amount of desired ease. Example: If your natural bust is 36 inches (91 cm) and you want 8 inches (20 cm) of positive ease, choose size 3.

Sample shown is knit in size 5.

MATERIALS

Yarn

- Bulky weight, KnitPicks® Biggo (50% superwash merino wool, 50% nylon), 110 yds (101 m) per 100-g (3.5 oz) skein

Yardage

- 590 (660, 730, 800, 850, 920) (990, 1050, 1120, 1200, 1250, 1350) yds / 540 (604, 668, 732, 777, 841) (905, 960, 1024, 1097, 1143, 1234) m

Shown In

- Dove Heather colorway

Any bulky weight yarn can be used for this pattern.

Needles

For cardigan

- US 13 (9 mm) 16-inch (40-cm), 24-inch (60-cm), and 32-inch (80-cm) circular needles, or size needed to obtain gauge

For picking up front band sts

- US 10 (6 mm) 24-inch (60-cm) circular needle, or three sizes smaller than your gauge needle

Notions

- 2 cable needles
- 8 stitch markers
- Tapestry needle
- Blocking materials

(continued)

GAUGE
10 sts & 14 rnds = 4 inches (10 cm) in stockinette st worked flat using larger needles (blocked)

SPECIAL TECHNIQUES
· Picking up and knitting stitches (page 170)

CABLE ABBREVIATIONS
All other abbreviations can be found on page 164.

· 1/1/1 LPC = 1/1/1 left purl cable
· 1/1/1 RPC = 1/1/1 right purl cable
· 1/1 LC = 1/1 left cable
· 1/1 RC = 1/1 right cable
· 1/2 LC = 1/2 left cable
· 1/2 RC = 1/2 right cable
· 1/3 LC = 1/3 left cable
· 1/3 RC = 1/3 right cable

SPECIAL STITCHES
· **1/1/1 LPC:** Sl next st to CN and place at front of work, sl next st to second CN and place at back of work, k1, p1 from back CN, then k1 from front CN.

· **1/1/1 RPC:** Sl next 2 sts to CN and place at back of work, k1, sl left-most st from CN to LH needle, move CN with rem st to front of work, p1 from LH needle, then k1 from CN.

· **1/1 LC:** Sl next st to CN and place at front of work, k1, then k1 from CN.

· **1/1 RC:** Sl next st to CN and place at back of work, k1, then k1 from CN.

· **1/2 LC:** Sl next st to CN and place at front of work, k2, then k1 from CN.

· **1/2 RC:** Sl next 2 sts to CN and place at back of work, k1, then k2 from CN.

· **1/3 LC:** Sl next st to CN and place at front of work, k3, then k1 from CN.

· **1/3 RC:** Sl next 3 sts to CN and place at back of work, k1, then k3 from CN.

· **LLI:** Lift the left leg of the st 2 rows below the st on RH needle onto LH needle and knit it through the back loop. [1 st increased]

· **RLI:** Lift right leg of the st below the next st on the LH needle onto the LH needle and knit it. [1 st increased]

Snow Fern Cardigan Pattern

NECK
With larger needle size, CO 29 (33, 35, 39, 43, 47) (49, 59, 59, 61, 67, 73) sts using a longtail cast-on.

SET-UP ROW (WS): P2 (3, 4, 5, 7, 8) (8, 10, 10, 10, 12, 14) for right front, pm, p5 (5, 5, 5, 5, 5) (5, 7, 7, 7, 7, 7) for right sleeve, pm, p15 (17, 17, 19, 19, 21) (23, 25, 25, 27, 29, 31) for back, pm, p5 (5, 5, 5, 5, 5) (5, 7, 7, 7, 7, 7) for left sleeve, pm, p2 (3, 4, 5, 7, 8) (8, 10, 10, 10, 12, 14) for left front. [4 markers placed]

Begin row 1 below working from the charts that are specific to the size that you are knitting (pages 40 to 55). When these charts end, all sizes transition to the main body charts for the fronts and back. **The size specific charts for front and back may or may not end on the same row. Therefore, you might be working on the size specific chart for the fronts and the main body chart for the back at the same time.** You will begin the main body charts on the row specified for your size, shown on the next page. Sleeves are worked in stockinette stitch and are not charted.

ROW 1 (RS RAGLAN INCREASE): Work Left Front Chart, LLI, sm, RLI, k to m, LLI, sm, RLI, work Back Chart, LLI, sm, RLI, k to m, LLI, sm, RLI, work Right Front Chart. [8 sts inc]

ROW 2 (WS): Work Right Front Chart, sm, p to m, sm, work Back Chart, sm, p to m, sm, work Left Front Chart.

Size-specific Front Charts completed after 22 (20, 18, 16, 12, 10) (10, 6, 6, 6, 2, 2) rows in total.

Size-specific Back Charts completed after 16 (14, 14, 12, 12, 10) (8, 6, 6, 4, 2, 2) rows in total.

TRANSITION TO MAIN BODY CHARTS
BEGIN ON:

Front Charts (Main Body) Row 13 (11, 9, 11, 7, 13) (13, 9, 9, 9, 5, 5)

Back Chart (Main Body) Row 7 (5, 5, 7, 7, 13) (11, 9, 9, 7, 5, 5)

ROWS 1–2 USING MAIN BODY CHARTS
ROW 1 (RS RAGLAN INCREASE): Work Left Front Chart, sm, k to raglan m, LLI, sm, RLI, k to raglan m, LLI, sm, RLI, k to chart m, sm, work Back Chart, sm, k to raglan m, LLI, sm, RLI, k to raglan m, LLI, sm, RLI, k to chart m, sm, work Right Front Chart.

ROW 2 (WS): Work Right Front Chart, sm, p to raglan m, sm, p to raglan m, sm, p to chart m, sm, work Back Chart, sm, p to raglan m, sm, p to raglan m, sm, p to chart m, sm, work Left Front Chart.

Working from charts as established and increasing at raglan markers every other row, repeat rows 1–2 until you have worked a total of 28 (30, 32, 34, 36, 38) (40, 42, 44, 46, 48, 50) rows, (this includes both size-specific and main body charts), ending after a WS row.

[141 (153, 163, 175, 187, 199) (209, 227, 235, 245, 259, 273) sts:

16 (18, 20, 22, 25, 27) (28, 31, 32, 33, 36, 39) front sts each;

33 (35, 37, 39, 41, 43) (45, 49, 51, 53, 55, 57) sleeve sts each;

43 (47, 49, 53, 55, 59) (63, 67, 69, 73, 77, 81) back sts]

SEPARATE SLEEVES FROM BODY
NEXT ROW (RS): Continuing charts as established, work Left Front Chart, sm, k to raglan m, remove marker. Place 33 (35, 37, 39, 41, 43) (45, 49, 51, 53, 55, 57) sleeve sts onto waste yarn, pm, CO 1 (1, 3, 3, 3, 3) (5, 5, 7, 9, 9, 9) sts for underarm, pm, k to chart m, sm, work Back Chart, sm, k to raglan m, remove marker. Place 33 (35, 37, 39, 41, 43) (45, 49, 51, 53, 55, 57) sleeve sts onto waste yarn, pm, CO 1 (1, 3, 3, 3, 3) (5, 5, 7, 9, 9, 9) sts for underarm, pm, k to chart m, sm, work Right Front Chart.

[77 (85, 95, 103, 111, 119) (129, 139, 147, 157, 167, 177) sts for Body]

BODY
Continue charts as established until your piece measures approximately 13 inches (33 cm) from underarm.

RIBBED HEM
SET-UP ROW (RS): Knit across row.

ROW 1 (WS): (P1, k1) across row.

ROW 2 (RS): (K1, p1) across row.

Work Rows 1–2 until hem measures 4 inches (10 cm). End on WS row.

Bind off on the RS in rib pattern.

COLLAR
Using smaller needle size and with RS facing, pu & k1 st from each cast-on st of the yoke.

[29 (33, 35, 39, 43, 47) (49, 59, 59, 61, 67, 73) sts]

Switch to larger needle size.

ROW 1 (WS): P2, (k1, p1) across to last st, p1.

ROW 2 (RS): K2, (p1, k1) across to last st, k1.

Work rows 1–2 for 2 inches (5 cm), ending with a WS row.

Bind off on the RS in rib pattern.

(continued)

Snow Fern Cardigan (Continued)

LEFT FRONT BAND
Beginning at the top edge of collar and with RS facing, use smaller needle size to pu & k3 sts from every 4 rows along the Left Front edge of cardigan, ending with an odd number of stitches. Switch to larger needle size.

ROW 1 (WS): P2, (k1, p1) across to last st, p1.

ROW 2 (RS): Sl1p wyif, (k1, p1) across to last 2 sts, k2.

Work rows 1–2 for 2½ (3, 3, 3½, 3½, 4) (4, 4, 4½, 4½, 4½, 4½, 4½) inches / 6.5 (7.5, 7.5, 9, 9, 10) (10, 10, 11.5, 11.5, 11.5, 11.5) cm, ending with a WS row.

Bind off on the RS in established rib pattern.

RIGHT FRONT BAND
Beginning at the bottom of the hem and with RS facing, use smaller needle size to pu & k3 sts from every 4 rows along the Right Front edge of cardigan, ending with an odd number of stitches.

Switch to larger needle size.

ROW 1 (WS): P2, (k1, p1) across to last st, p1.

ROW 2 (RS): Sl1p wyif, (k1, p1) across to last 2 sts, k2.

Work Rows 1–2 for 2½ (3, 3, 3½, 3½, 4) (4, 4, 4½, 4½, 4½, 4½, 4½) inches / 6.5 (7.5, 7.5, 9, 9, 10) (10, 10, 11.5, 11.5, 11.5, 11.5) cm, ending with a WS row.

Bind off on the RS in established rib pattern.

SLEEVES (MAKE BOTH THE SAME)
Using the larger needle size, place sleeve sts from waste yarn onto 16-inch (40-cm) circular or DPNs.

RND 1: With RS facing, pu & k1 st from the center CO st of the 3 sts at underarm, pu & k1 st on the next CO, knit across all sleeve sts, pu & k1 st from the first CO at underarm. Pm for BOR. [36 (38, 40, 42, 44, 46) (48, 52, 54, 56, 58, 60) sts]

RND 2 (DECREASE ARMPIT): K1, k2tog, k to last 2 sts, ssk. [34 (36, 38, 40, 42, 44) (46, 50, 52, 54, 56, 58) sts]

Knit in the round without decreasing until sleeve measures 15 inches (38 cm) from armpit.

CUFF
SIZES - (2, -, 4, -, 6) (-, -, 9, -, 11, -)
DECREASE: K2tog around.

SIZES 1 (-, 3, -, 5, -) (7, 8, -, 10, -, 12)
DECREASE: K2, *k2tog* to end.

ALL SIZES: [18 (18, 20, 20, 22, 22) (24, 26, 26, 28, 28, 30) sts]

RND 1: (K1, p1) around.

Work rnd 1 until cuff measures 4 inches (10 cm).

Bind off loosely in rib pattern.

FINISHING
Block cardigan to finished dimensions. Once completely dry, unpin and weave in all ends.

Snow Fern Cardigan Schematic

Back Neck Width: 6 (6¾, 6¾, 7½, 7½, 8½) (9¼, 10, 10, 10¾, 11½, 12½)"/ 15 (17, 17, 19, 19, 21.5) (23, 25, 25, 27, 29, 31) cm

Back Width at Underarm: 17¼ (18¾, 19½, 21¼, 22, 23½) (25¼, 26¾, 27½, 29¼, 30¾, 32½)" / 43 (47, 49, 53, 55, 59) (64, 67, 69, 74, 78, 82.5) cm

Upper Sleeve Circumference: 13½ (14½, 15¼, 16, 16¾, 17½) (18½, 20, 20¾, 21½, 22½, 23¼)"/ 34 (37, 39, 41, 43, 44) (47, 51, 53, 55, 57, 59) cm

Yoke Depth: 8 (8½, 9¼, 9¾, 10¼, 10¾) (11½, 12, 12½, 13¼, 13¾, 14¼)" / 20 (21.5, 23, 24.5, 26, 27) (29, 30, 31.5, 33.5, 35, 36) cm

Sleeve Length from Underarm: 19" / 48 cm

Underarm Cast-On Width: ½ (½, 1¼, 1¼, 1¼, 1¼) (2, 2, 2¾, 3½, 3½, 3½)" / 1 (1, 3, 3, 3, 3) (5, 5, 7, 9, 9, 9) cm

Cuff Circumference: 7¼ (7¼, 8, 8, 8¾, 8¾) (9½, 10½, 10½, 11¼, 11¼, 12)"/ 18 (18, 20, 20, 22, 22) (24, 27, 27, 29, 29, 30) cm

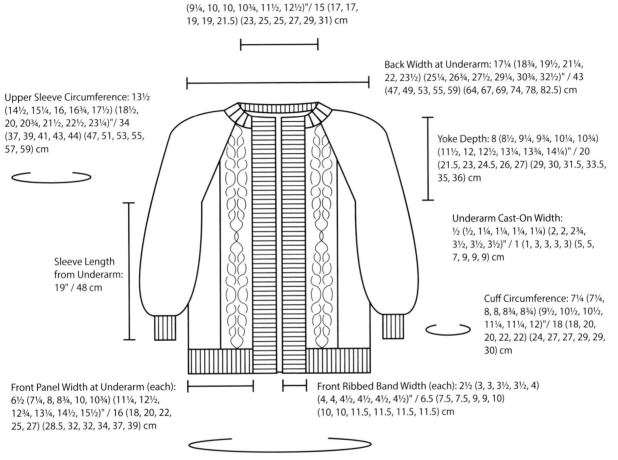

Front Panel Width at Underarm (each): 6½ (7¼, 8, 8¾, 10, 10¾) (11¼, 12½, 12¾, 13¼, 14½, 15½)" / 16 (18, 20, 22, 25, 27) (28.5, 32, 32, 34, 37, 39) cm

Front Ribbed Band Width (each): 2½ (3, 3, 3½, 3½, 4) (4, 4, 4½, 4½, 4½, 4½)" / 6.5 (7.5, 7.5, 9, 9, 10) (10, 10, 11.5, 11.5, 11.5, 11.5) cm

Bust Circumference (including front ribbed bands): 35¾ (40, 44, 48¼, 51½, 55½) (59½, 63½, 67¾, 71¾, 75¾, 79¾)" / 91 (101.5, 112, 122.5, 131, 141) (151, 161, 172, 182, 192.5, 202.5) cm

Snow Fern Cardigan Chart Key

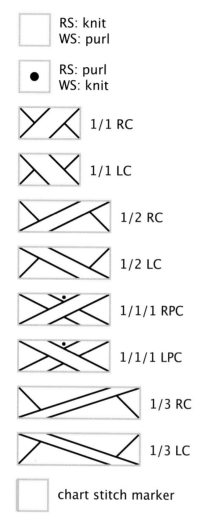

RS: knit
WS: purl

RS: purl
WS: knit

1/1 RC

1/1 LC

1/2 RC

1/2 LC

1/1/1 RPC

1/1/1 LPC

1/3 RC

1/3 LC

chart stitch marker

Snow Fern Cardigan Left Front Chart (Main Body)

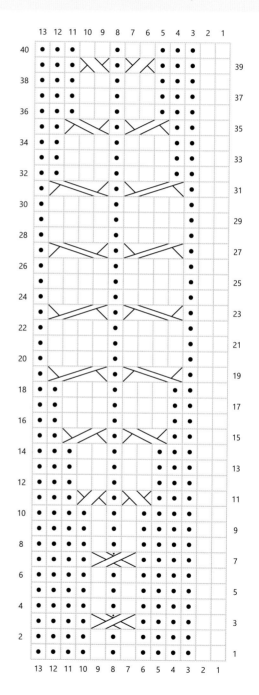

Snow Fern Cardigan Back Chart (Main Body)

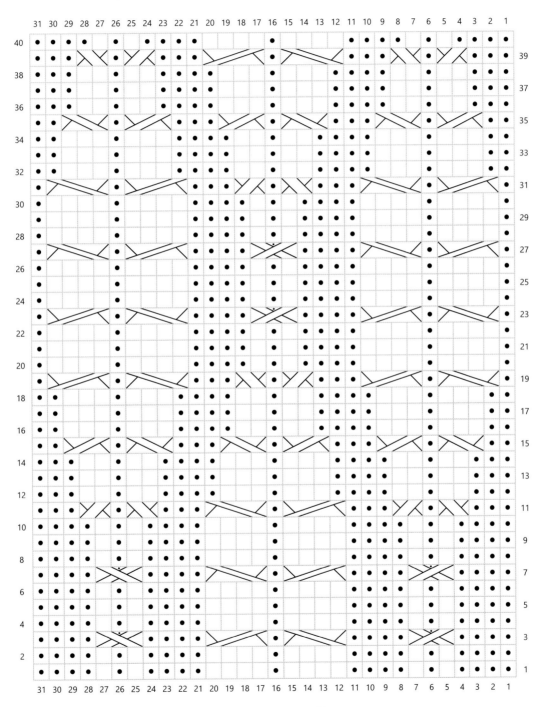

Snow Fern Cardigan Right Front Chart (Main Body)

Snow Fern Cardigan Left Front Shoulder Chart (Size 1)

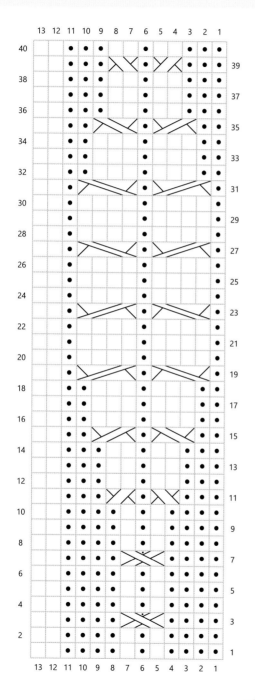

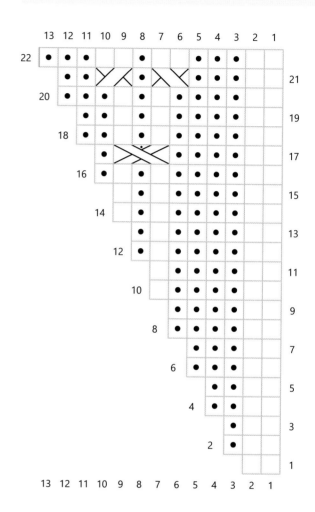

Snow Fern Cardigan Back Shoulder Chart (Size 1)

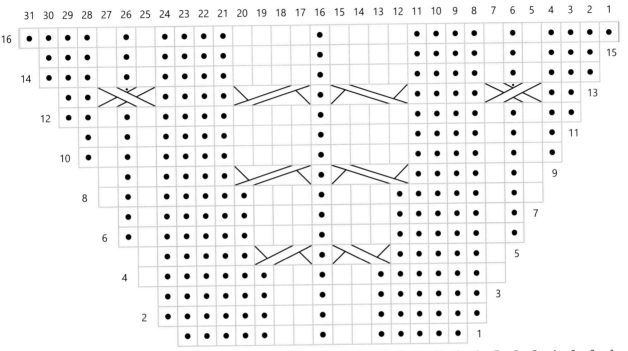

Snow Fern Cardigan Right Front Shoulder Chart (Size 1)

Snow Fern Cardigan Left Front Shoulder Chart (Size 2)

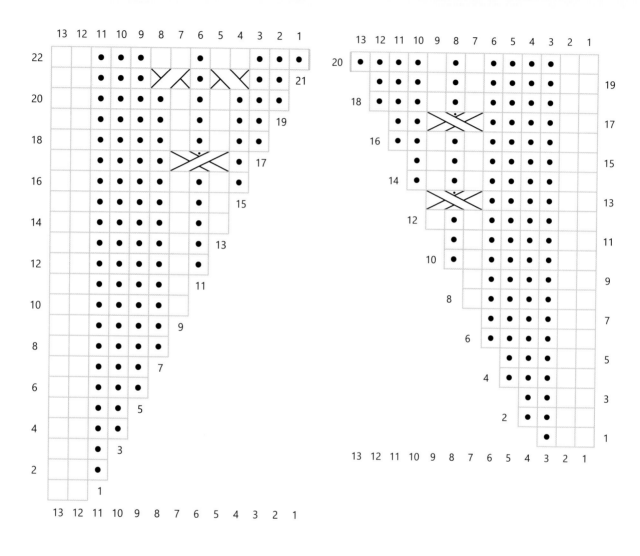

Snow Fern Cardigan Back Shoulder Chart (Size 2)

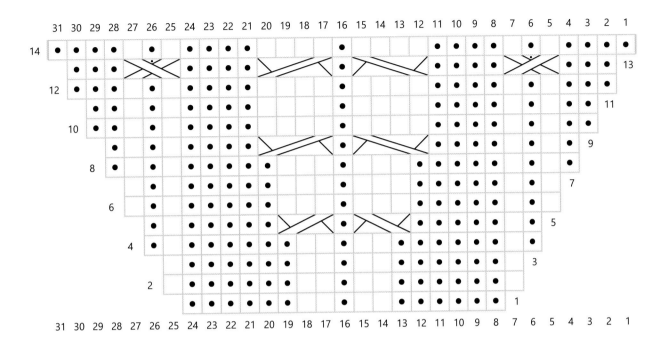

Snow Fern Cardigan Right Front Shoulder Chart (Size 2)

Snow Fern Cardigan Left Front Shoulder Chart (Size 3)

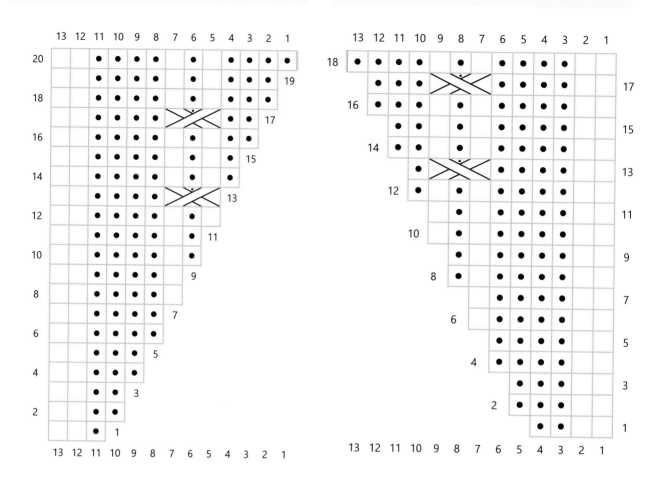

Snow Fern Cardigan Back Shoulder Chart (Size 3)

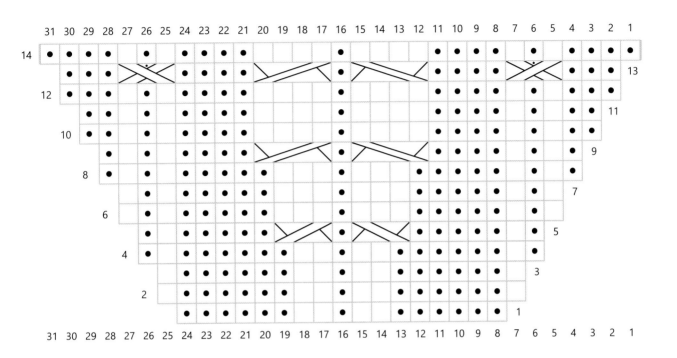

Snow Fern Cardigan Right Front Shoulder Chart (Size 3)

Snow Fern Cardigan Left Front Shoulder Chart (Size 4)

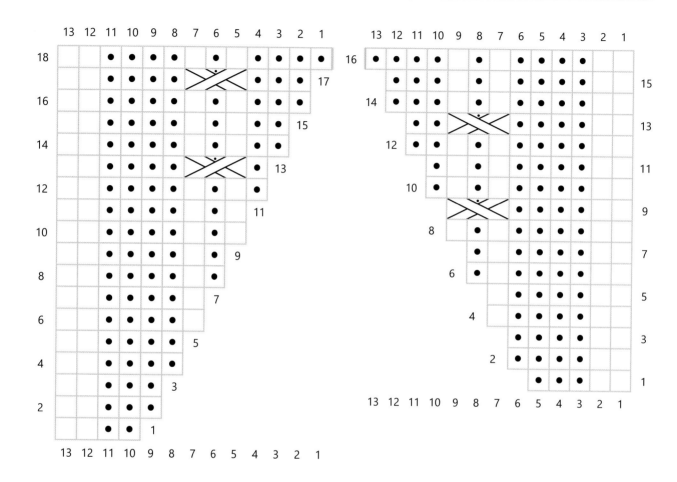

Snow Fern Cardigan Back Shoulder Chart (Size 4)

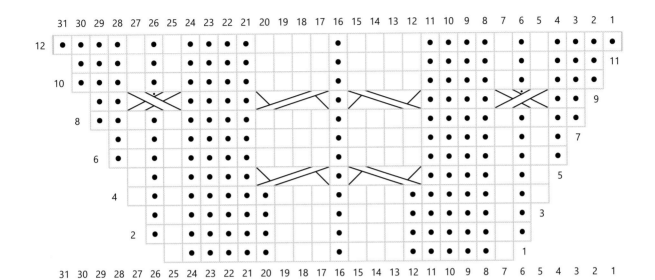

Snow Fern Cardigan Right Front Shoulder Chart (Size 4)

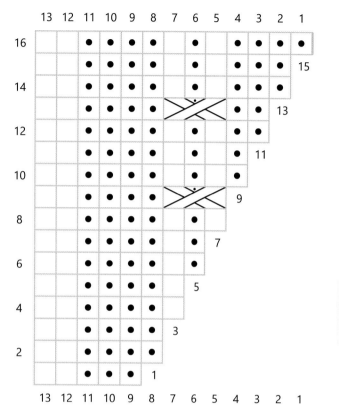

Snow Fern Cardigan Left Front Shoulder Chart (Size 5)

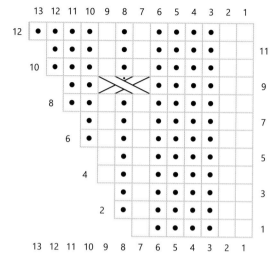

Snow Fern Cardigan Right Front Shoulder Chart (Size 5)

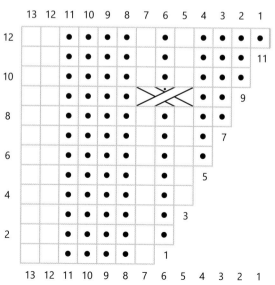

Snow Fern Cardigan Back Shoulder Chart (Size 5)

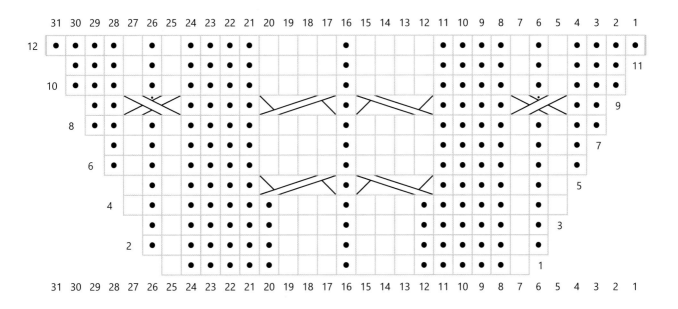

Snow Fern Cardigan Left Front Shoulder Chart (Size 6)

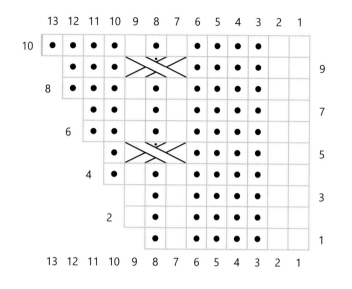

Snow Fern Cardigan Right Front Shoulder Chart (Size 6)

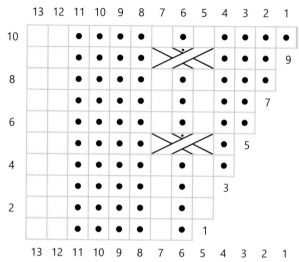

Snow Fern Cardigan Back Shoulder Chart (Size 6)

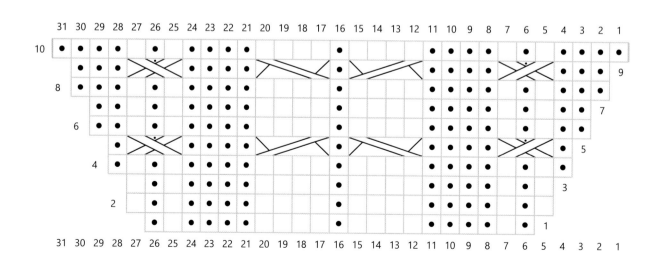

Snow Fern Cardigan Left Front Shoulder Chart (Size 7)

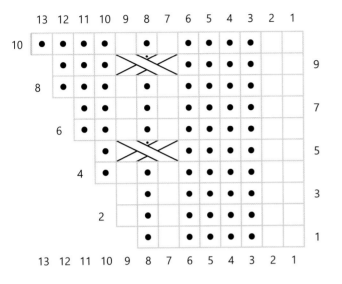

Snow Fern Cardigan Right Front Shoulder Chart (Size 7)

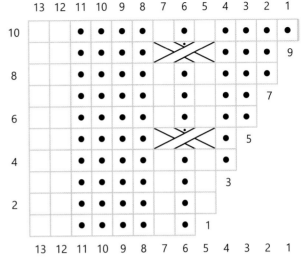

Snow Fern Cardigan Back Shoulder Chart (Size 7)

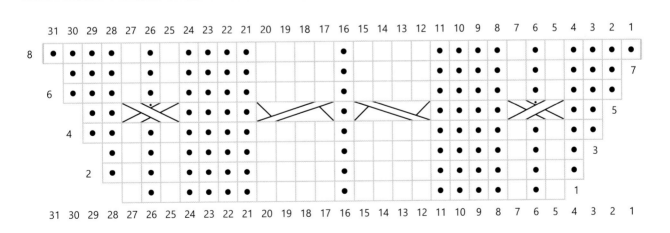

Snow Fern Cardigan Left Front Shoulder Chart (Sizes 8 & 9)

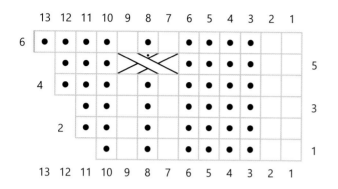

Snow Fern Cardigan Right Front Shoulder Chart (Sizes 8 & 9)

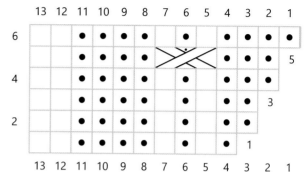

Snow Fern Cardigan Back Shoulder Chart (Sizes 8 & 9)

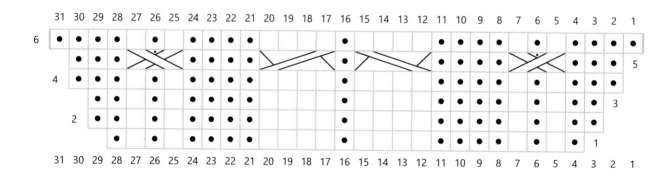

Snow Fern Cardigan Left Front Shoulder Chart (Size 10)

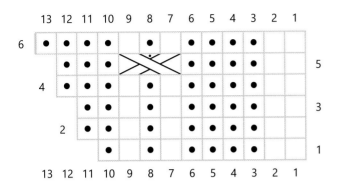

Snow Fern Cardigan Right Front Shoulder Chart (Size 10)

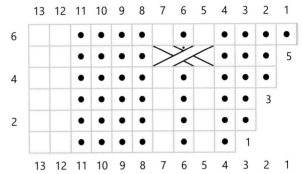

Snow Fern Cardigan Back Shoulder Chart (Size 10)

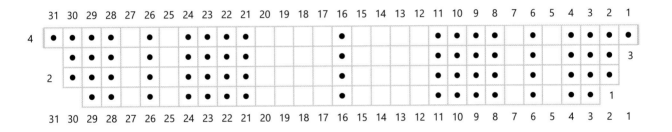

Snow Fern Cardigan Left Front Shoulder Chart (Size 11)

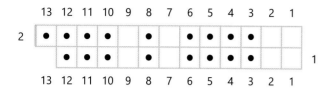

Snow Fern Cardigan Right Front Shoulder Chart (Size 11)

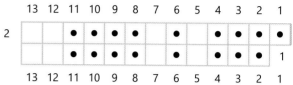

Snow Fern Cardigan Back Shoulder Chart (Size 11)

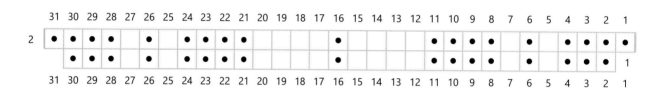

Snow Fern Cardigan Left Front Shoulder Chart (Size 12)

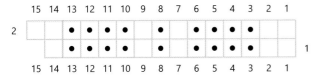

Snow Fern Cardigan Right Front Shoulder Chart (Size 12)

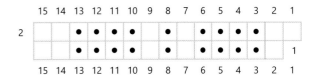

Snow Fern Cardigan Back Shoulder Chart (Size 12)

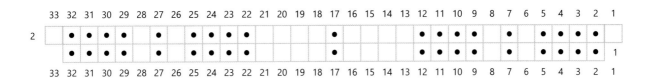

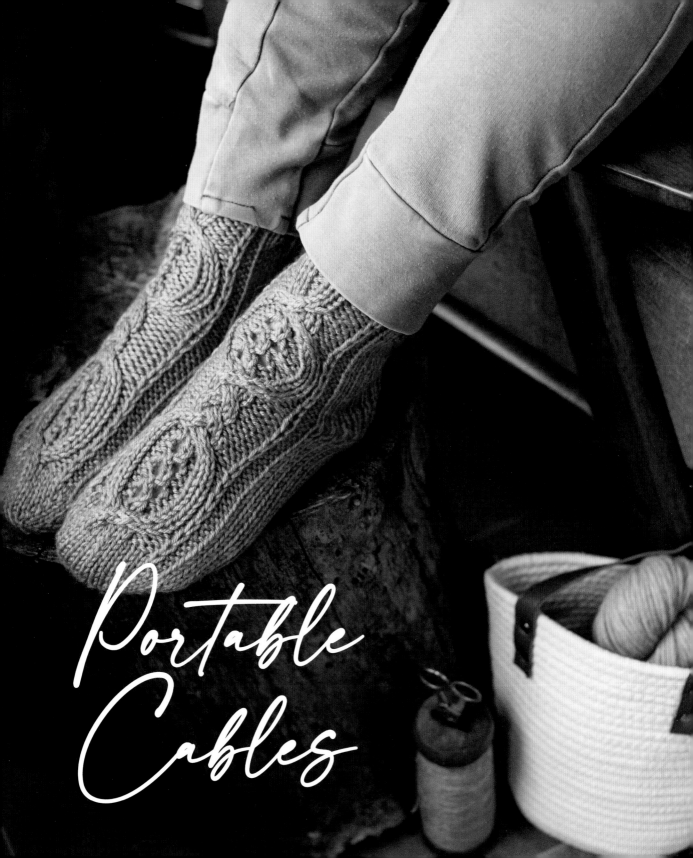

Portable
Cables

FOR GRAB-AND-GO KNITTING. SMALL-SCALE PROJECTS WITH EASY-TO-MEMORIZE CABLE PATTERNS.

In this chapter, you will find projects that travel well. Small and portable, with stitch patterns that repeat with ease, these projects include socks, a hat, a headband and a button-up cowl.

This selection is a great go-to for long trips or doctors' appointments. Busy your hands and your mind with any of these portable projects, as you choose from patterns that all include a cable repeat you can set on cruise control. Easy to commit to memory, you can put your project down one week and pick it back up another without losing your rhythm.

Smokestack Ankle Socks

These socks are inspired by the smokestack we would drive by on breezy fall trips to the Oregon coast when I was a child. Wide, oval-shaped cables enwrap inserts of winding lace that mimic the smoke billowing out of the smokestack. This is the perfect portable project to work on in just a day or two, and only one skein of Universal® Uptown Worsted is needed to make a pair. Work them with the Magic Loop method for an easy, no-fuss, on-the-go knitting project. This pattern is charted and includes written instructions for both the right sock and the left sock.

CONSTRUCTION

These socks are worked in the round from the toe up. Judy's Magic Cast-on begins these socks and shadow wrap short rows make up the heel. The pattern is written using the Magic Loop method but DPNs can also be used. The pattern will direct you on how to distribute the stitches. Written in one adult size but additional stockinette stitches can be added for extra width. The footbed is adjustable from a women's size 8 to 10.

SKILL LEVEL

Complex

SIZE

US women's size 8 to 10

Finished circumference:

7 inches (18 cm), blocked

Finished length:

11½ inches (29 cm), blocked

Foot length is adjustable.

MATERIALS

Yarn

Aran weight, Universal® Uptown Worsted (100% anti-pilling acrylic), 180 yds (165 m) per 100-g skein

Yardage

150 yards (137 m)

Shown In

351 Latte colorway (1 skein)

Any Aran weight yarn can be used for this pattern.

Needles

For sock

US 8 (5 mm) 32-inch (80-cm) circular needle or 4 DPNs, or size needed to obtain gauge

For toe & cuff

US 7 (4.5 mm) 32-inch (80-cm) circular needle, or one size down from needle you meet gauge with

Notions

- 2 cable needles
- Stitch markers
- Tapestry needle
- Blocking materials

GAUGE

18 sts x 24 rnds = 3½ x 4 inches (9 x 10 cm) in cable pattern in the round using larger needle (blocked)

SPECIAL TECHNIQUES

- Judy's Magic Cast-on (page 167)
- Shadow wrap knit (page 171)
- Shadow wrap purl (page 171)
- Twin stitch (page 171)
- Triplet stitch (page 171)

(continued)

CABLE ABBREVIATIONS

All other abbreviations can be found on page 164.

- 2/2 LC = 2/2 left cable
- 2/2 LPC = 2/2 left purl cable
- 2/2 RC = 2/2 right cable
- 2/2 RPC = 2/2 right purl cable
- 2/2/2 LPC = 2/2/2 left purl cable
- 2/2/2 RPC = 2/2/2 right purl cable
- 2/4 LC = 2/4 left cable
- 2/4 RC = 2/4 right cable

SPECIAL STITCHES

- **2/2 LC:** Sl next 2 sts to CN and place at front of work, k2, then k2 from CN.

- **2/2 LPC:** Sl next 2 sts to CN and place at front of work, p2, then k2 from CN.

- **2/2 RC:** Sl next 2 sts to CN and place at back of work, k2, then k2 from CN.

- **2/2 RPC:** Sl next 2 sts to CN and place at back of work, k2, then p2 from CN.

- **2/2/2 LPC:** Sl next 2 sts to CN and place at front of work, sl next 2 sts to second CN and place at back of work, k2, p2 from back CN, then k2 from front CN.

- **2/2/2 RPC:** Sl next 4 sts to CN and place at back of work, k2, sl 2 left-most sts from CN to LH needle, move CN with rem sts to front of work, p2 from LH needle, then k2 from CN.

- **2/4 LC:** Sl next 2 sts to CN and place at front of work, k4, then k2 from CN.

- **2/4 RC:** Sl next 4 sts to CN and place at back of work, k2, then k4 from CN.

- **M1L:** With the LH needle, pick up the bar between the st you knit and the one you're about to knit, bringing the needle from front to back. Next, insert the tip of the right needle purlwise into the back leg of the strand and knit as usual. [1 st increased]

- **M1R:** With the LH needle, pick up the bar between the st you knit and the one you're about to knit, bringing the needle from back to front. Next, insert the tip of the right needle knitwise into the front leg of the strand and knit as usual. [1 st increased]

Smokestack Ankle Socks Pattern

Note: For Magic Loop, half of the sts should be on the front needle and the other half should be on the back needle. If working on 4 DPNs, needles 1 & 2 will be referenced in the pattern as the front needle and needles 3 & 4 will be referenced as the back needle.

TOE

With smaller needles, CO 16 sts using Judy's Magic Cast-on. Join in the round.

RND 1: Knit.

RND 2: (K1, m1R, k to last st on needle, m1L, k1) 2 times. [4 sts increased]

Work rnds 1–2 until you have 36 sts on your needles.

Knit 1 rnd.

FOOT

Note: Work both socks the same but use the corresponding charts (page 64) for the right and left sock.

The front needle (or DPN 1 & 2) will hold sts for the instep (charted). The back needle (or DPN 3 & 4) will hold sole sts. The sole sts are uncharted and will always be worked in stockinette stitch.

Using larger needles, and following the correct chart for right or left, work until the sock measures 3 inches (7.5 cm) shorter than the actual foot length. Make a note of which chart row you end on, so you can begin again on the correct row.

HEEL

Note: Work heel on back needle (or DPN 3 & 4) only.

SHORT ROW 1 (RS): K17, swk, turn.

SHORT ROW 2 (WS): P16, swp, turn.

SHORT ROW 3: K15, swk, turn.

SHORT ROW 4: P14, swp, turn.

SHORT ROW 5: K13, swk, turn.

SHORT ROW 6: P12, swp, turn.

SHORT ROW 7: K11, swk, turn.

SHORT ROW 8: P10, swp, turn.

SHORT ROW 9: K9, swk, turn.

SHORT ROW 10: P8, swp, turn.

SHORT ROW 11: K7, swk, turn.

SHORT ROW 12: P6, swp, turn.

There will be 6 unworked sts in the middle with 6 shadow wraps (twin sts) on each side. [18 sts]

SHORT ROW 13: K6, k twin st as 1 st, swk twin st, turn.

SHORT ROW 14: P7, p twin st as 1 st, swp twin st, turn.

SHORT ROW 15: K8, k triplet st as 1 st, swk twin st, turn.

SHORT ROW 16: P9, p triplet st as 1 st, swp twin st, turn.

SHORT ROW 17: K10, k triplet st as 1 st, swk twin st, turn.

SHORT ROW 18: P11, p triplet st as 1 st, swp twin st, turn.

SHORT ROW 19: K12, k triplet st as 1 st, swk twin st, turn.

SHORT ROW 20: P13, p triplet st as 1 st, swp twin st, turn.

SHORT ROW 21: K14, k triplet st as 1 st, swk twin st, turn.

SHORT ROW 22: P15, p triplet st as 1 st, swp twin st, turn.

SHORT ROW 23: K16, k triplet as 1 st. Do not turn.

Note: The shadow wrap left at the beginning of the final short row will be worked as 1 st on the next rnd of the sock.

ANKLE
Begin working in the rnd again, continuing with your chart where you ended before the heel. Work through the last rnd of the chart.

CUFF
Switch to smaller needle size.

Note: For a looser ankle, keep using the larger needle size.

RND 1: P2, k1, p3, k2, p2, k2, p3, k1, (p2, k2) 5 times.

RND 2: P2, sl1p wyib, p3, k2, p2, k2, p3, sl1p wyib, (p2, k2) 5 times.

RNDS 3–6: Repeat rnds 1–2 twice more.

BIND OFF
Bind off loosely in pattern.

FINISHING
Weave in ends and block to finished measurements.

(continued)

Smokestack Ankle Socks Right Sock Chart Instructions

RND 1: P2, sl1p wyib, p3, 2/2 LC, k2, p3, sl1p wyib, p2. [18 sts]

RND 2: P2, k1, p3, k6, p3, k1, p2.

RND 3: P2, sl1p wyib, p1, 2/2 RPC, 2/2/2 LPC, p1, sl1p wyib, p2.

RND 4: P2, k1, p1, (k2, p2) 2 times, k2, p1, k1, p2.

RND 5: P2, sl1p wyib, p1, k2, p2, yo, ssk, p2, k2, p1, sl1p wyib, p2.

RND 6: Rep rnd 4.

RND 7: P2, sl1p wyib, p1, k2, p2, k2tog, yo, p2, k2, p1, sl1p wyib, p2.

RNDS 8 – 15: Rep rnds 4-7 twice.

RND 16: Rep rnd 4.

RND 17: P2, sl1p wyib, p1, 2/2 LPC, 2/4 RC, p1, sl1p wyib, p2.

RND 18: Rep rnd 2.

RND 19: Rep rnd 1.

RND 20: Rep rnd 2.

RND 21: P2, sl1p wyib, p3, k2, 2/2 RC, p3, sl1p wyib, p2.

RNDS 22 – 25: Rep rnds 18-21.

RND 26: Rep rnd 2.

RND 27: Rep rnd 1.

RND 28: Rep rnd 2.

RND 29: Rep rnd 3.

RND 30: Rep rnd 4.

RND 31: Rep rnd 5.

RND 32: Rep rnd 4.

RND 33: Rep rnd 7.

RNDS 34 – 41: Rep rnds 30-33 twice.

RND 42: Rep rnd 4.

RND 43: Rep rnd 17.

RND 44: Rep rnd 2.

RND 45: Rep rnd 1.

RND 46: Rep rnd 2.

RND 47: P2, sl1p wyib, p3, k2, 2/2 LPC, p3, sl1p wyib, p2.

Smokestack Ankle Socks Left Sock Chart Instructions

RND 1: P2, sl1p wyib, p3, k2, 2/2 RC, p3, sl1p wyib, p2. [18 sts]

RND 2: P2, k1, p3, k6, p3, k1, p2.

RND 3: P2, sl1p wyib, p1, 2/2/2 RPC, 2/2 LPC, p1, sl1p wyib, p2.

RND 4: P2, k1, p1, (k2, p2) 2 times, k2, p1, k1, p2.

RND 5: P2, sl1p wyib, p1, k2, p2, k2tog, yo, p2, k2, p1, sl1p wyib, p2.

RND 6: Rep rnd 4.

RND 7: P2, sl1p wyib, p1, k2, p2, yo, ssk, p2, k2, p1, sl1p wyib, p2.

RNDS 8 – 15: Rep rnds 4-7 twice.

RND 16: Rep rnd 4.

RND 17: P2, sl1p wyib, p1, 2/4 LC, 2/2 RPC, p1, sl1p wyib, p2.

RND 18: Rep rnd 2.

RND 19: Rep rnd 1.

RND 20: Rep rnd 2.

RND 21: P2, sl1p wyib, p3, 2/2 LC, k2, p3, sl1p wyib, p2.

RNDS 22 – 25: Rep rnds 18-21.

RND 26: Rep rnd 2.

RND 27: Rep rnd 1.

RND 28: Rep rnd 2.

RND 29: Rep rnd 3.

RND 30: Rep rnd 4.

RND 31: Rep rnd 5.

RND 32: Rep rnd 4.

RND 33: Rep rnd 7.

RNDS 34 – 41: Rep rnds 30–33 twice.

RND 42: Rep rnd 4.

RND 43: Rep rnd 17.

RND 44: Rep rnd 2.

RND 45: Rep rnd 1.

RND 46: Rep rnd 2.

RND 47: P2, sl1p wyib, p3, 2/2 RPC, k2, p3, sl1p wyib, p2.

Smokestack Ankle Socks
Schematic

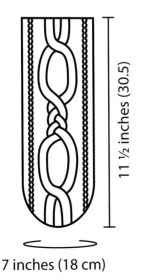

11 ½ inches (30.5)

7 inches (18 cm)

Smokestack Ankle Socks
Chart Key

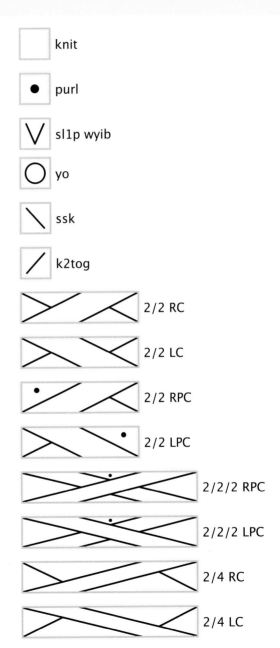

knit

• purl

V sl1p wyib

O yo

\ ssk

/ k2tog

2/2 RC

2/2 LC

2/2 RPC

2/2 LPC

2/2/2 RPC

2/2/2 LPC

2/4 RC

2/4 LC

Smokestack Ankle Socks
Chart (Right)

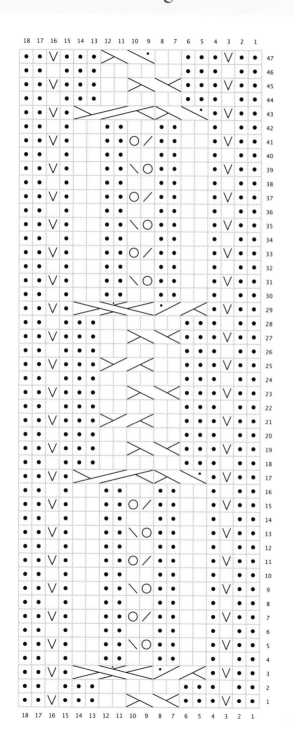

Smokestack Ankle Socks
Chart (Left)

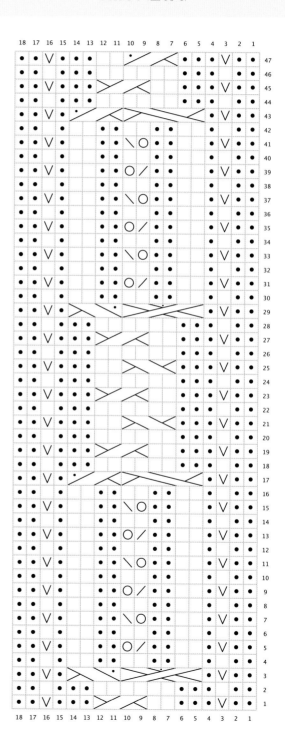

Snowberry Hat

This hat is inspired by the frozen berry bushes that decorate the landscape in the snowy Blue Mountains in Washington and Oregon. Snowberry is a deceptively simple design. Try your hand at the easiest cable there is, with 2-stitch cables that create the winding branches on this beautiful project. Bobbles introduce a fun element to break up any monotony and keep your interest piqued. This pattern is charted and includes written instructions.

CONSTRUCTION

Snowberry is worked in the round from the brim up, with a 1x1 rib that creates a wonderfully stretchy brim that will fit a wide range of head sizes. Cabled branches and bobbles travel along a reverse stockinette background in the body of the hat.

SKILL LEVEL

Intermediate

SIZE

One size

FINISHED MEASUREMENTS

17 inches (43 cm) circumference x 9 inches (23 cm) height, blocked

MATERIALS

Yarn

Worsted weight, Malabrigo Worsted (100% Merino wool), 210 yds (192 m) per 100 g-skein

Yardage

160 yards (146 m)

Shown In

Pearl colorway (1 skein)

Any worsted weight yarn can be used for this pattern.

Needles

For body

US 8 (5 mm) 16-inch (40-cm) circular needle, or size needed to obtain gauge

For crown

US 8 (5 mm) DPNs, or size needed to obtain gauge

For brim

US 7 (4.5 mm) 16-inch (40-cm) circular needle, or one size down from needle you make gauge with

Notions

Cable needle

Stitch markers

Tapestry needle

Blocking materials

GAUGE

20 sts x 29 rnds = 4 inches (10 cm) in cable pattern in the round, using larger needle (blocked)

SPECIAL TECHNIQUE

Bobbles (page 165)

CABLE ABBREVIATIONS

All other abbreviations can be found on page 164.

1/1 RC = 1/1 right cable

1/1 LC = 1/1 left cable

1/1 RPC = 1/1 right purl cable

1/1 LPC = 1/1 left purl cable

(continued)

SPECIAL STITCHES

- **1/1 RC:** Sl next st to CN and place at back of work, k1, then k1 from CN.
- **1/1 LC:** Sl next st to CN and place at front of work, k1, then k1 from CN.
- **1/1 RPC:** Sl next st to CN and place at back of work, k1, then p1 from CN.
- **1/1 LPC:** Sl next st to CN and place at front of work, p1, then k1 from CN.
- **CDD:** Worked over 3 sts. Insert RH needle through two sts from left to right knitwise, sl these sts off the needle, k1, then pass sl sts over the knit st. [3 sts decreased to 1]

Snowberry Hat Pattern

HAT BRIM

With smaller needles, CO 84 sts using a longtail cast-on. Join in the round. Pm for BOR.

RND 1: (K1, P1) 42 times.

Work rnd 1 until work measures 1½ inches (4 cm) from cast-on.

HAT BODY

Using larger needles, work rnds 1–42 of Snowberry Hat Chart (page 69).

HAT CROWN

Note: Switch to DPNs when needed.

RND 1: (1/1 RPC, mb, p1, p2tog, k1, p2tog, p5) 6 times. [72 sts]

RND 2: (K1, p4, k1, p6) 6 times.

RND 3: (Mb, p2, p2tog, k1, p2tog, p4) 6 times. [60 sts]

RND 4: (P4, k1, p5) 6 times.

RND 5: (P2, p2tog, k1, p2tog, p3) 6 times. [48 sts]

RND 6: (P3, k1, p4) 6 times.

RND 7: (P1, p2tog, k1, p2tog, p2) 6 times. [36 sts]

RND 8: (P2, k1, p3) 6 times.

RND 9: (P2tog, k1, p2tog, p1) 6 times. [24 sts]

RND 10: (P1, k1, p2) 6 times.

RND 11: (CDD, p1) 6 times. [12 sts]

RND 12: (K1, p1) 6 times.

FINISHING

Break yarn and pass through the 12 rem sts, using a tapestry needle. Pull tightly and secure with a knot inside the hat. Weave in ends and block to finished dimensions.

(continued)

Snowberry Hat Chart Instructions

RND 1: (P5, 1/1 RC, p7) 6 times.

RND 2: (P5, k2, p7) 6 times.

RND 3: (P4, 1/1 RPC, k1, p7) 6 times.

RND 4: (P4, k1, p1, k1, p7) 6 times.

RND 5: (P3, 1/1 RPC, p1, k1, p7) 6 times.

RND 6: (P3, k1, p2, k1, p7) 6 times.

RND 7: (P1, mb, 1/1 RPC, p2, k1, p7) 6 times.

RND 8: (P2, k1, p3, k1, p7) 6 times.

RND 9: (Mb, 1/1 RPC, mb, p2, 1/1 LC, p6) 6 times.

RND 10: (P1, k1, p4, k2, p6) 6 times.

RND 11: (1/1 RPC, mb, p3, k1, 1/1 LPC, p5) 6 times.

RND 12: (K1, p5, k1, p1, k1, p5) 6 times.

RND 13: (Mb, p5, k1, p1, 1/1 LPC, p4) 6 times.

RND 14: (P6, k1, p2, k1, p4) 6 times.

RND 15: (P6, k1, p2, 1/1 LPC, mb, p2) 6 times.

RND 16: [P6, (k1, p3) 2 times] 6 times.

RND 17: (P5, 1/1 RC, p2, mb, 1/1 LPC, mb, p1) 6 times.

RND 18: (P5, k2, p4, k1, p2) 6 times.

RND 19: (P4, 1/1 RPC, k1, p3, mb, 1/1 LPC, p1) 6 times.

RND 20: (P4, k1, p1, k1, p5, k1, p1) 6 times.

RND 21: (P3, 1/1 RPC, p1, k1, p5, mb, p1) 6 times.

RNDS 22 – 37: Rep rnds 6-21.

RNDS 38 – 40: Rep rnds 6-8.

RND 41: (Mb, 1/1 RPC, mb, p2, k1, p7) 6 times.

RND 42: (P1, k1, p4, k1, p7) 6 times.

Snowberry Hat Schematic

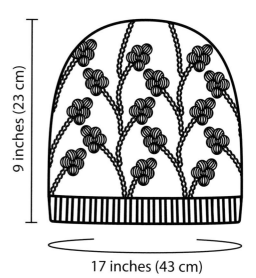

9 inches (23 cm)

17 inches (43 cm)

Snowberry Hat Chart Key

knit

• purl

⦿ bobble

X⟋ 1/1 RC

⟍X 1/1 LC

•⟋ 1/1 RPC

X• 1/1 LPC

14–st repeat

Snowberry Hat Chart

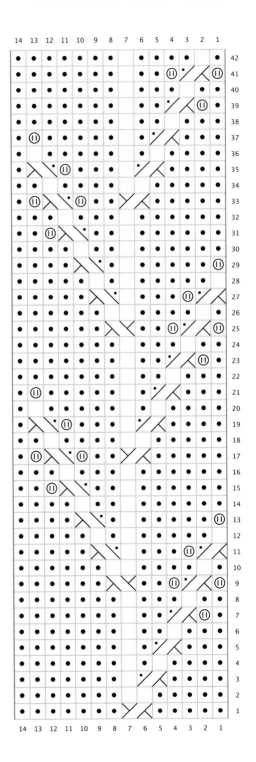

Snow Tracks Headband

Snow Tracks features a simple but striking cable that gives the illusion of downhill ski impressions in the fresh snow. Delicate bobbles are encased between the cables, mimicking snowballs rolling downhill between the tracks. This is an ideal project for portable, on-the-go knitting. The band of garter stitch at the back of the headband is slightly wider for ease of wear and optimal stretch. For a larger circumference, add more row repeats. This pattern is charted and includes written instructions.

CONSTRUCTION

This headband is worked back and forth on straight needles and then seamed together using a 3-needle bind-off. You'll also need some waste yarn in a matching weight for the provisional cast-on.

SKILL LEVEL

Intermediate

SIZE

One size to fit adult head size 16 to 23 inches (40.5 to 58.5 cm)

FINISHED MEASUREMENTS

4 inches (10 cm) wide x 16 inches (40.5 cm) circumference, blocked

MATERIALS

Yarn

Worsted weight, Woolfolk Far (100% Ovis 21 Ultimate Merino®), 142 yds (130 m) per 50-g skein

Yardage

70 yards (64 m)

Shown In

Colorway 01 (1 skein)

Any worsted weight yarn can be used for this pattern.

Needles

For headband

US 7 (4.5 mm) straight needles, or size needed to obtain gauge

For 3-needle bind-off

One US 7 (4.5 mm) DPN, or size needed to obtain gauge

Notions

US 7 (4.5 mm) crochet hook

Cable needle

Tapestry needle

Blocking materials

GAUGE

23 sts & 24 rows = 4 inches (10 cm) in cable pattern worked flat (blocked)

SPECIAL TECHNIQUES

Provisional cast-on (page 170)

3-needle bind-off (page 165)

Bobbles (page 165)

CABLE ABBREVIATIONS

All other abbreviations can be found on page 164.

2/2 LC = 2/2 left cable

2/2 RC = 2/2 right cable

SPECIAL STITCHES

2/2 LC: Sl next 2 sts to CN and place at front of work, k2, then k2 from CN.

2/2 RC: Sl next 2 sts to CN and place at back of work, k2, then k2 from CN.

(continued)

Snow Tracks Headband (Continued)

Snow Tracks Headband Pattern

CO 23 sts using a provisional cast-on.

ROW 1 (WS): Knit

ROW 2 (RS): Knit

Work rows 1–2 for 2½ inches (6.5 cm). End with a WS row.

Work rows 1–4 of Snow Tracks Headband Chart (page 73) once.

Work rows 5–10 of Snow Tracks Headband Chart for approximately 11 inches (28 cm). End with a row 10.

Work rows 11–13 of Snow Tracks Headband Chart once.

Work rows 1–2 for 2½ inches (6.5 cm).

SEAM HEADBAND
Remove provisional cast-on, placing live sts onto a second needle.

Fold piece with WS facing, meeting the top and bottom rows of sts together. Using the DPN, work a 3-needle bind-off.

FINISHING
Weave in all ends. Turn headband to RS and steam block to finished measurements.

Snow Tracks Headband Chart Instructions

ROW 1 (RS): K5, p1, k4, p3, k4, p1, k5.

ROW 2 (WS): K6, p4, k3, p4, k6.

ROWS 3 – 4: Rep rows 1–2.

ROW 5: K5, p1, 2/2 RC, p1, mb, p1, 2/2 LC, p1, k5.

ROW 6: K6, p4, k3, p4, k6.

ROW 7: K5, p1, k4, p3, k4, p1, k5.

ROWS 8 – 9: Rep rows 6–7.

ROW 10: Rep row 6.

ROW 11: K5, p1, 2/2 RC, p1, mb, p1, 2/2 LC, p1, k5.

ROW 12: Rep row 2.

ROW 13: Rep row 1.

Snow Tracks Headband Schematic

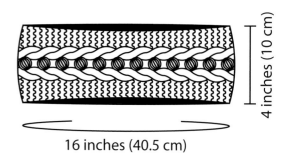

4 inches (10 cm)

16 inches (40.5 cm)

Snow Tracks Headband Chart Key

	RS: knit WS: purl
•	RS: purl WS: knit
⦅Ⅱ⦆	bobble
⧅	2/2 RC
⧅	2/2 LC
—	6-row repeat

Snow Tracks Headband Chart

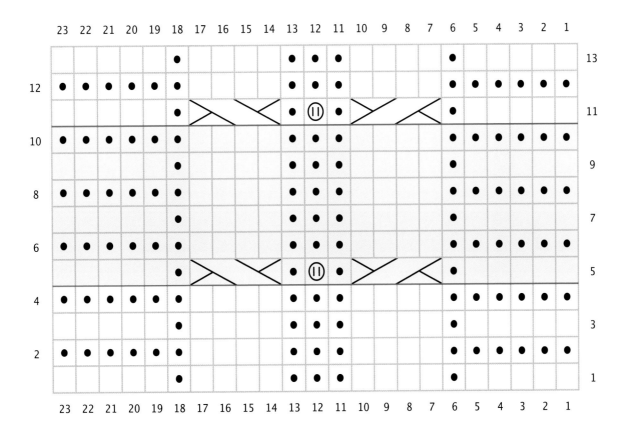

Ice Chalet Cowl

This design harkens back to trips to the ski lodge when I was a child. I would stare out the frosted windows with their Swiss chalet–shaped panes as I sipped my cocoa. The Ice Chalet Cowl will keep you toasty out on the slopes or inside the ski chalet. It features a center cable panel that travels outward and inward over a slipped stitch background. An icy-cool effect is achieved with complex cable stitches. Dip your toes into some crochet techniques like slip stitches and chains with the button band and loops. But please feel free to omit this finishing step and use frog-style closures to complete your cowl. This pattern is charted and includes written instructions.

CONSTRUCTION

This cowl is worked back and forth on straight needles. The ribbing is picked up next and the button band and loops are created last with a crochet hook. Again, feel free to omit this finishing step and use frog-style closures to complete your cowl instead.

SKILL LEVEL
- Complex

SIZE
- One size

FINISHED MEASUREMENTS
- 9½ x 26 inches (24 x 66 cm), blocked

MATERIALS

Yarn
- Bulky weight, Woolfolk Luft (55% Ovis 21 Ultimate Merino, 45% organic Pima cotton), 109 yds (100 m) per 50-g skein

Yardage
- 210 yards (192 m)

Shown In
- L8 colorway (2 skeins)

Any bulky weight yarn can be used for this pattern.

Needles
- US 10½ (6.5 mm) 32-inch (80-cm) circular needle, or size needed to obtain gauge

Notions
- 2 cable needles
- US K-10.5 (6.5 mm) crochet hook (optional)
- 5 (1-inch [2.5-cm]) toggle buttons
- Locking stitch marker
- Tapestry needle
- Blocking materials

GAUGE
- 33 sts & 8 rows = 1½ x 7 inches (4 x 10 cm) in one cable pattern repeat, worked flat (blocked)

SPECIAL TECHNIQUES
- Picking up and knitting stitches (page 170)
- Crochet slip stitch (page 166)
- Crochet chain (page 165)

CABLE ABBREVIATIONS

All other abbreviations can be found on page 164.
- 2/1/2 LC = 2/1/2 left cable
- 2/1/2 RC = 2/1/2 right cable
- 2/1/2 RPC = 2/1/2 right purl cable
- 2/2 LPC = 2/2 left purl cable
- 2/2 RPC = 2/2 right purl cable

(continued)

SPECIAL STITCHES

- **2/1/2 LC:** Sl next 2 sts to CN and place at front of work, sl next st to CN and place at back of work, k2, k1 from back CN, then k2 from front CN.
- **2/1/2 RC:** Sl next 3 sts to CN and place at back of work, k2, sl left-most st from CN to LH needle, move CN with rem sts to front of work, k1 from LH needle, then k2 from CN.
- **2/1/2 RPC:** Sl next 3 sts to CN and place at back of work, k2, sl left-most st from CN to LH needle, move CN with rem sts to front of work, p1 from LH needle, then k2 from CN.
- **2/2 LPC:** Sl next 2 sts to CN and place at front of work, p2, then k2 from CN.
- **2/2 RPC:** Sl next 2 sts to CN and place at back of work, k2, then p2 from CN.

Ice Chalet Cowl Pattern

CO 35 sts using a longtail cast-on.

BODY

Work rows 1–9 of Ice Chalet Chart (page 79) once. [9 rows]

Work rows 10–17 of Ice Chalet Chart a total of 15 times. [120 rows]

Work rows 18–25 of Ice Chalet Chart once. [8 rows]

BO in established pattern on the RS, leaving the last bind-off loop on needle. Rotate work so that you'll be working along the left side of the cowl, with the RS facing you.

NECK RIBBING

Note: You'll be picking up stitches behind the slipped stitches from the cowl.

You have 1 loop on your needle left from your BO, this counts as your first stitch.

Skip the first row, *pu & k3 sts from the next 3 rows, skip 1 row; rep from * 33 more times, pu & k1 st in last row. [104 sts] Turn work.

ROW 1 (WS): Sl1p wyif, p2, (k2, p2) to the last st, k1.

ROW 2 (RS): Sl1p wyif, (k2, p2) to the last 3 sts, k3.

ROW 3: Rep row 1.

ROW 4: Rep row 2.

ROW 5: Rep row 1.

BO on the RS in pattern. Do not break yarn. Insert a locking stitch marker through the final BO loop. Measure out 3 yards (3 m) of your working yarn and cut.

COLLAR RIBBING

Rotate work to the opposite long edge of the cowl. Using working yarn, pu & k104 sts as you did on the opposite edge. Work exactly as with the neck ribbing through row 5.

BO on the RS in established pattern. Do not break yarn. Place the rem BO loop onto crochet hook. Tighten up the loop.

CROCHET BUTTON LOOPS

Sl st in the next 2 sl sts alongside the rib rows, sl st in the center of the sl st of the cowl, ch6, sl st in the same st you previously sl st into, sl st in the next 7 BO loops, ch6, sl st in the same st you previously sl st into, *sl st in the next 10 BO loops, ch6, sl st in the same st you previously sl st into; rep from * once more, sl st in the next 6 BO loops, sl st in the center of the sl st of the cowl, ch6, sl st in the same st you previously sl st into, sl st in the 2 sl sts along the rib rows, break yarn and pull through the loop on hook. Work a seamless join.

SEAMLESS JOIN

Weave the yarn tail through a tapestry needle and insert the needle through both loops (from front to back) of the very first BO loop of the collar ribbing, then pass the needle back down through the last loop that the tail was coming out of. You've now created a seamless finish to your crochet loop edge. [5 total button loops made]

CROCHET BUTTON BAND

Rotate work so that opposite short edge of cowl (CO edge) is at the top, RS facing you. Remove locking stitch marker from the BO loop and place this loop onto your crochet hook. You will now begin working with the reserved 3 yards (3 m) of yarn left over from your neck ribbing BO.

Sl st in the next 2 sl sts of the rib rows, sl st in the center of the sl st from the cowl, sl st in the next 33 CO loops, sl st in the center of the sl st from the cowl, sl st in the last 2 sl sts alongside the ribbed rows. Break yarn and pull through rem loop on hook. Weave the yarn tail through a tapestry needle and create a seamless join as you did on the other side of the cowl.

FINISHING

Weave in all ends. Lightly steam block to finished dimensions. Sew toggles onto the flat edge side of the cowl, using the corresponding button loops as a guide.

Ice Chalet Cowl Chart Instructions

ROW 1 (WS): Sl1p wyif, k4, (p2, k1, p2, k2, p1, k2) 2 times, p2, k1, p2, k5.

ROW 2 (RS): Sl1p wyif, p4, (k2, p1, k2, p2, sl1p wyib, p2) 2 times, k2, p1, k2, p4, k1.

ROW 3: Rep row 1.

ROWS 4 – 5: Rep rows 2–3.

ROW 6: Sl1p wyif, p4, (2/1/2 RC, p2, sl1p wyib, p2) 2 times, 2/1/2 RC, p4, k1.

ROW 7: Sl1p wyif, k4, (p5, k2, p1, k2) 2 times, p5, k5.

ROW 8: Sl1p wyif, p2, (2/2 RPC, sl1p wyib, 2/2 LPC, sl1p wyib) 2 times, 2/2 RPC, sl1p wyib, 2/2 LPC, p2, k1.

ROW 9: Sl1p wyif, k2, p2, (k2, p1, k2, p5) 2 times, k2, p1, k2, p2, k3.

ROW 10: Sl1p wyif, p2, k2, (p2, sl1p wyib, p2, 2/1/2 LC) 2 times, p2, sl1p wyib, p2, k2, p2, k1.

ROW 11: Rep row 9.

ROW 12: Sl1p wyif, p2, (2/2 LPC, sl1p wyib, 2/2 RPC, sl1p wyib) 2 times, 2/2 LPC, sl1p wyib, 2/2 RPC, p2, k1.

ROW 13: Rep row 7.

ROWS 14 – 21: Rep rows 6–13.

ROW 22: Sl1p wyif, p4, (2/1/2 RPC, p2, sl1p wyib, p2) 2 times, 2/1/2 RPC, p4, k1.

ROW 23: Rep row 1.

ROW 24: Rep row 2.

ROW 25: Rep row 1.

Ice Chalet Cowl Schematic

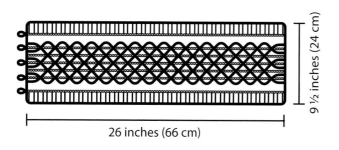

9 ½ inches (24 cm)

26 inches (66 cm)

Ice Chalet Cowl Chart Key

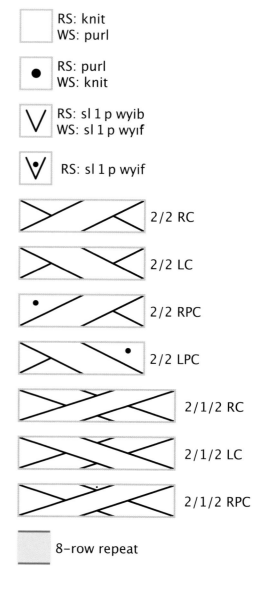

RS: knit
WS: purl

RS: purl
WS: knit

RS: sl 1 p wyib
WS: sl 1 p wyif

RS: sl 1 p wyif

2/2 RC

2/2 LC

2/2 RPC

2/2 LPC

2/1/2 RC

2/1/2 LC

2/1/2 RPC

8-row repeat

Ice Chalet Cowl Chart

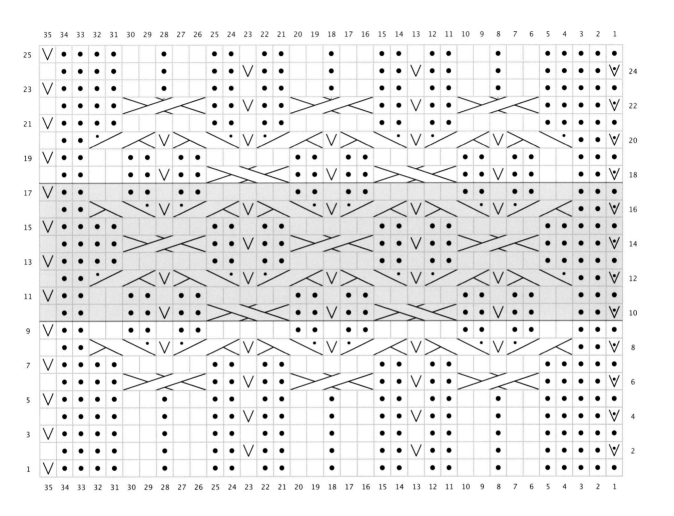

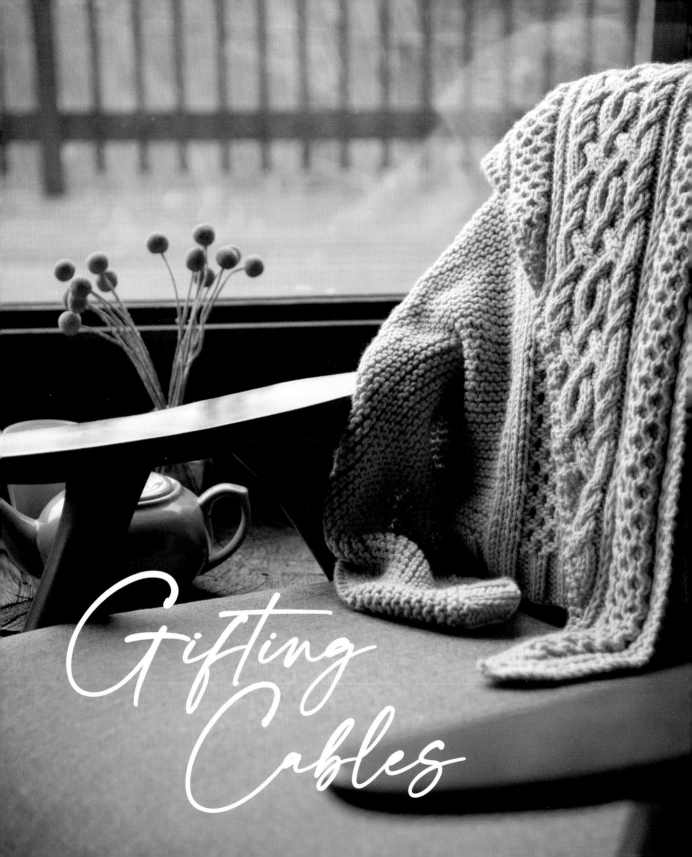

Gifting Cables

PATTERNS FOR THOSE NEAR AND DEAR.
MORE THOUGHTFUL STITCH PATTERNS
AND INTRICATE CABLES.

Looking for the perfect gift for someone special in your life? Look no further than these four patterns for gifting. Choose from a pair of cabled mitts, a matching hat, a striking asymmetric shawl or a big, cozy throw. Whether you're looking for a small project or a large one, from graduations and housewarmings to weddings and anniversaries, these patterns will give you a great set of choices.

I've included some more complex cable designs that include twisted-stitch cables, honeycomb cables and I also snuck in a little lace and fun bobbles to mix things up and keep your interest piqued. I hope you'll reach for these patterns often when knitting for friends and loved ones.

Campfire Stories Hat

This design evokes memories from my youth, vacationing in the mountains with family. We would sit around the campfire on cool fall evenings, beneath a starry sky. The intertwined cables travel up into the air like smoke and flame from the crackling fire. The eyelet lace represents the tops of pines that stand tall and proud in the forest. This pattern is charted and includes written instructions.

CONSTRUCTION

Campfire Stories is worked in the round with twisted cables and bands of simple lace. A stretchy German twisted longtail cast-on is utilized, allowing this hat to fit a wide range of head sizes.

SKILL LEVEL

- Complex

SIZES

- One size

FINISHED MEASUREMENTS

- 18 inches (46 cm) circumference x 9 inches (23 cm) tall, blocked

MATERIALS

Yarn

- Worsted weight, Malabrigo Rios (100% superwash Merino wool), 210 yds (192 m) per 100-g skein

Yardage

- 200 yards (183 m)

Shown In

- Pearl colorway (1 skein)

Any worsted weight yarn can be used for this pattern.

Needles

For body

- US 7 (4.5 mm) 16-inch (40-cm) circular needle, or size needed to obtain gauge

For crown

- US 7 (4.5 mm) DPNs, or size needed to obtain gauge

For brim

- US 6 (4 mm) 16-inch (40-cm) circular needle, or one size smaller than size needed to obtain gauge

Notions

- 2 cable needles
- Stitch markers
- Tapestry needle
- Blocking materials

GAUGE

- 20 sts x 19 rnds = 3 inches (7.5 cm) in cable pattern in the round using larger needle (blocked)
- 20 sts x 19 rnds = 3 inches (7.5 cm) in 1x1 rib in the round using smaller needle (blocked)

SPECIAL TECHNIQUES

- German twisted longtail cast-on (page 166)

(continued)

CABLE ABBREVIATIONS

All other abbreviations can be found on page 164.

- 3/2 RTC = 3/2 right twist cable
- 3/2 LTC = 3/2 left twist cable
- 3/2 RTPC = 3/2 right twist purl cable
- 3/2 LTPC = 3/2 left twist purl cable
- 3/1/3 RTC = 3/1/3 right twist cable
- 3/1/3 LTC = 3/1/3 left twist cable

SPECIAL STITCHES

- **3/2 RTC:** Sl next 2 sts to CN and place at back of work, k1tbl, p1, k1tbl, then p1, k1tbl from CN.
- **3/2 LTC:** Sl next 3 sts to CN and place at front of work, k1tbl, p1, then k1tbl, p1, k1tbl from CN.
- **3/2 RTPC:** Sl next 2 sts to CN and place at back of work, k1tbl, p1, k1tbl, then p2 from CN.
- **3/2 LTPC:** Sl next 3 sts to CN and place at front of work, p2, then k1tbl, p1, k1tbl from CN.
- **3/1/3 RTC:** Sl next 4 sts to CN and place at back of work, k1tbl, p1, k1tbl, sl left-most st from CN to LH needle, move CN with rem sts to front of work, p1 from LH needle, then k1tbl, p1, k1tbl from CN.
- **3/1/3 LTC:** Sl next 3 sts to CN and place at front of work, sl next st to second CN and place at back of work, k1tbl, p1, k1tbl; p1 from back CN, then k1tbl, p1, k1tbl from front CN.

Campfire Stories Hat Pattern

HAT BRIM

With smaller needle, CO 120 sts using German twisted longtail cast-on. Join in the round. Place unique marker for BOR.

Work rnds 1–8 of Campfire Stories Hat Chart (pages 88–91).

HAT BODY

Note: Place a stitch marker after first chart repeat.

Using larger needle, work rnds 9–57 of Campfire Stories Hat Chart. When finished, your work should measure approximately 8½ inches (21 cm).

HAT CROWN

Note: Remove repeat marker. Switch to DPNs when needed.

RND 1: K2togtbl 60 times. [60 sts]

RND 2: K1tbl 60 times.

RND 3: K2togtbl 30 times. [30 sts]

RND 4: K1tbl 30 times.

RND 5: K2togtbl 15 times. [15 sts]

FINISHING

Break yarn and pass through the 15 rem sts, using a tapestry needle. Pull tightly and secure with a knot inside the hat. Weave in ends and block to finished dimensions.

Campfire Stories Hat Chart Instructions

RNDS 1 – 8: (K1tbl, p1) 60 times.

RND 9: *Yo, ssk, k1tbl, k2tog, yo, (p1, k1tbl) 4 times, p1, 3/1/3 RTC, (p1, k1tbl) 4 times, p1, yo, ssk, k1tbl, k2tog, yo, (p1, k1tbl) 4 times, p1, 3/1/3 LTC, (p1, k1tbl) 4 times, p1; repeat from * once more.

RND 10: *K2, k1tbl, k2, (p1, k1tbl) 12 times, p1; repeat from * 3 more times.

RND 11: *K1, yo, sk2p, yo, k1, (p1, k1tbl) 3 times, p1, 3/2 RTPC, p1, 3/2 LTPC, (p1, k1tbl) 3 times, p1; repeat from * 3 more times.

RND 12: *K5, (p1, k1tbl) 5 times, p5, (k1tbl, p1) 5 times; repeat from * 3 more times.

RND 13: *Yo, ssk, k1, k2tog, yo, p1, k1tbl, p1, 3/1/3 RTC, p5, 3/1/3 LTC, p1, k1tbl, p1; repeat from * 3 more times.

RND 14: Repeat rnd 12.

RND 15: *K1, yo, sk2p, yo, k1, (p1, 3/2 RTPC, p1, 3/2 LTPC) 2 times, p1; repeat from * 3 more times.

RND 16: *K5, [(p1, k1tbl) 2 times, p5, k1tbl, p1, k1tbl] 2 times, p1; repeat from * 3 more times.

RND 17: *Yo, ssk, k1, k2tog, yo, (p1, k1tbl) 2 times, p5, 3/1/3 RTC, p5, (k1tbl, p1) 2 times, yo, ssk, k1, k2tog, yo, (p1, k1tbl) 2 times, p5, 3/1/3 LTC, p5, (k1tbl, p1) 2 times; repeat from * once more.

RND 18: Repeat rnd 16.

RND 19: *K1, yo, sk2p, yo, k1, [(p1, k1tbl) 2 times, (p5, k1tbl, p1, k1tbl) 2 times, p1] 2 times; repeat from * 3 more times.

RND 20: *K5, [(p1, k1tbl) 2 times, p2, mb, p2, k1tbl, p1, k1tbl] 2 times, p1; repeat from * 3 more times.

RND 21: *Yo, ssk, k1, k2tog, yo, [(p1, k1tbl) 2 times, p5, k1tbl, p1, k1tbl] 2 times, p1; repeat from * 3 more times.

RND 22: Repeat rnd 16.

RND 23: *K1, yo, sk2p, yo, k1, (p1, k1tbl) 2 times, p5, 3/1/3 RTC, p5, (k1tbl, p1) 2 times, k1, yo, sk2p, yo, k1, (p1, k1tbl) 2 times, p5, 3/1/3 LTC, p5, (k1tbl, p1) 2 times; repeat from * once more.

RND 24: Repeat rnd 16.

RND 25: *Yo, ssk, k1, k2tog, yo, (p1, 3/2 LTPC, p1, 3/2 RTPC) 2 times, p1; repeat from * 3 more times.

RND 26: *K5, p3, (k1tbl, p1) 3 times, k1tbl, p5, (k1tbl, p1) 3 times, k1tbl, p3; repeat from * 3 more times.

RND 27: *K1, yo, sk2p, yo, k1, p3, 3/1/3 LTC, p5, 3/1/3 RTC, p3; repeat from * 3 more times.

RND 28: Repeat rnd 26.

RND 29: *Yo, ssk, k1, k2tog, yo, p3, (k1tbl, p1) 3 times, k1tbl, p5, (k1tbl, p1) 3 times, k1tbl, p3; repeat from * 3 more times.

RND 30: *K5, p3, (k1tbl, p1) 3 times, k1tbl, p2, mb, p2, (k1tbl, p1) 3 times, k1tbl, p3; repeat from * 3 more times.

(continued)

RND 31: *K1, yo, sk2p, yo, k1, p3, (k1tbl, p1) 3 times, k1tbl, p5, (k1tbl, p1) 3 times, k1tbl, p3; repeat from * 3 more times.

RND 32: Repeat rnd 26.

RND 33: *Yo, ssk, k1, k2tog, yo, p3, 3/1/3 LTC, p5, 3/1/3 RTC, p3; repeat from * 3 more times.

RND 34: Repeat rnd 26.

RND 35: Repeat rnd 15.

RND 36: Repeat rnd 16.

RND 37: Repeat rnd 17.

RND 38: Repeat rnd 16.

RND 39: Repeat rnd 19.

RND 40: Repeat rnd 20.

RND 41: Repeat rnd 21.

RND 42: Repeat rnd 16.

RND 43: Repeat rnd 23.

RND 44: Repeat rnd 16.

RND 45: *Yo, ssk, k1, k2tog, yo, p1, 3/2 LTC, p1, 3/2 RTPC, p1, 3/2 LTPC, p1, 3/2 RTC, p1; repeat from * 3 more times.

RND 46: Repeat rnd 12.

RND 47: *K1, yo, sk2p, yo, k1, p1, k1tbl, p1, 3/1/3 LTC, p5, 3/1/3 RTC, p1, k1tbl, p1; repeat from * 3 more times.

RND 48: Repeat rnd 12.

RND 49: *Yo, ssk, k1, k2tog, yo, (p1, k1tbl) 3 times, p1, 3/2 LTC, p1, 3/2 RTC, (p1, k1tbl) 3 times, p1; repeat from * 3 more times.

RND 50: *K5, (p1, k1tbl) 12 times, p1; repeat from * 3 more times.

RND 51: *Ktbl, yo, sk2p, yo, (k1tbl, p1) 5 times, 3/1/3 RTC, (p1, k1tbl) 5 times, yo, sk2p, yo, (k1tbl, p1) 5 times, 3/1/3 LTC, (p1, k1tbl) 4 times, p1; work from * once more.

RNDS 52 – 57: (K1tbl, p1) 60 times.

Campfire Stories Hat Schematic

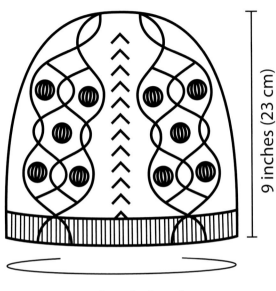

9 inches (23 cm)

18 inches (46 cm)

Campfire Stories Hat Chart Key

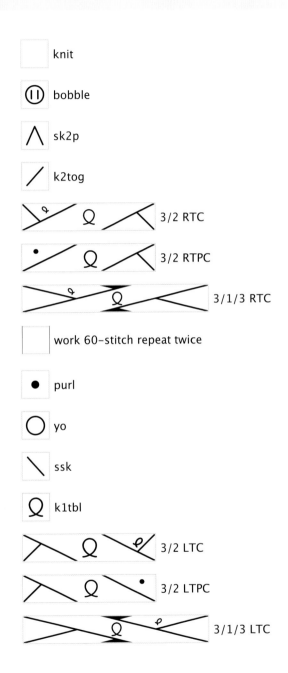

knit

bobble

sk2p

k2tog

3/2 RTC

3/2 RTPC

3/1/3 RTC

work 60-stitch repeat twice

purl

yo

ssk

k1tbl

3/2 LTC

3/2 LTPC

3/1/3 LTC

Campfire Stories Hat Chart (Bottom Left)

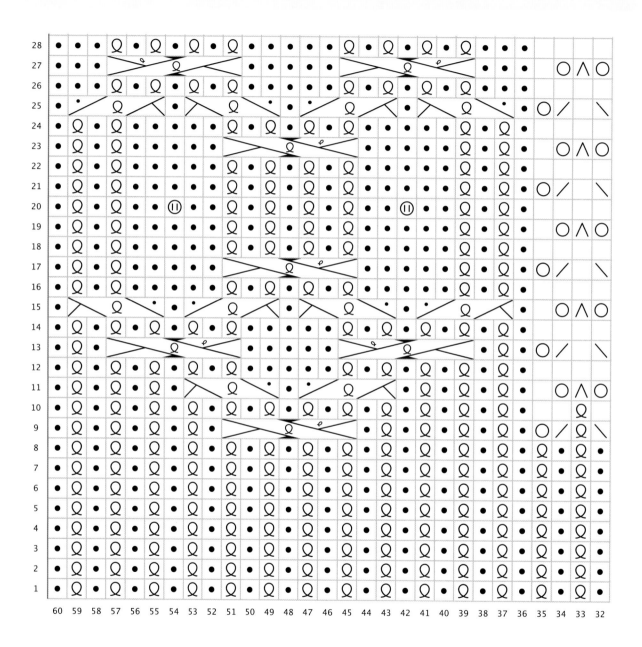

Campfire Stories Hat Chart (Bottom Right)

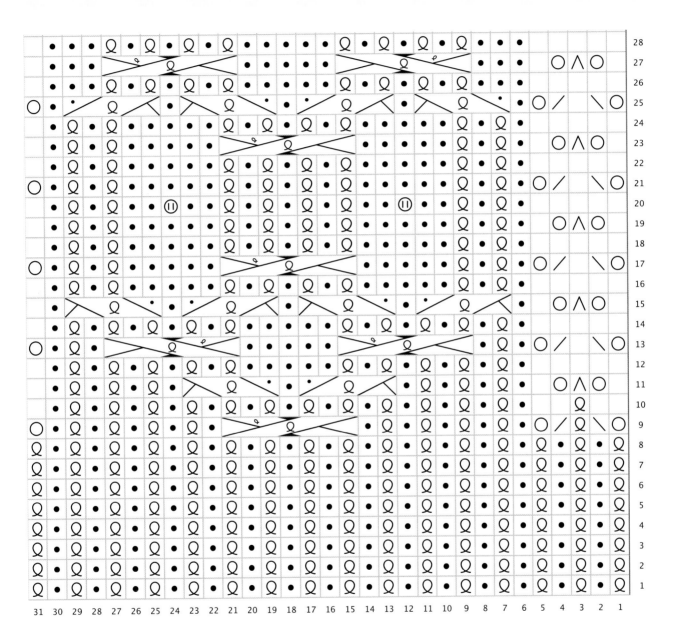

Campfire Stories Hat Chart (Top Left)

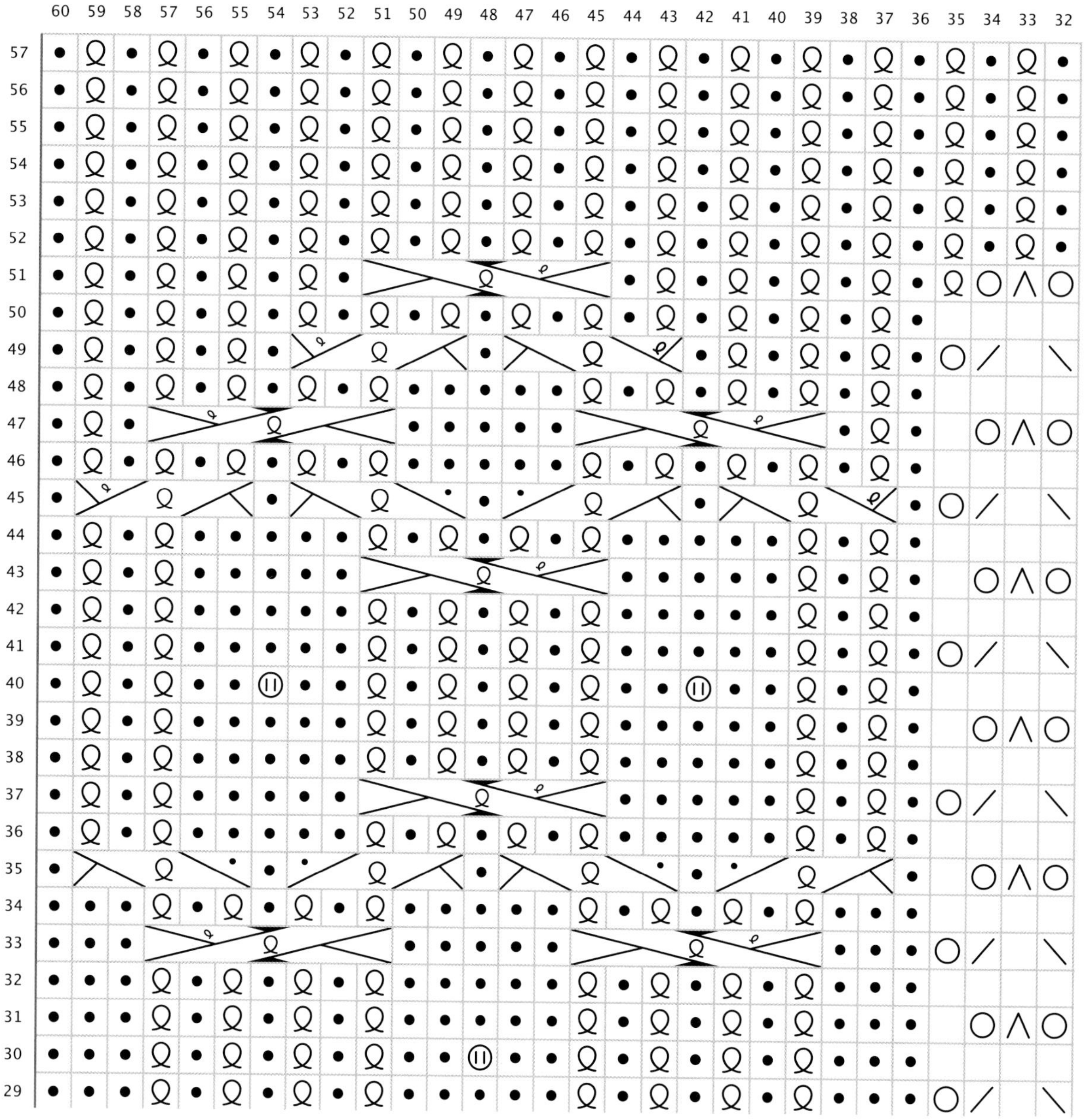

Campfire Stories Hat Chart (Top Right)

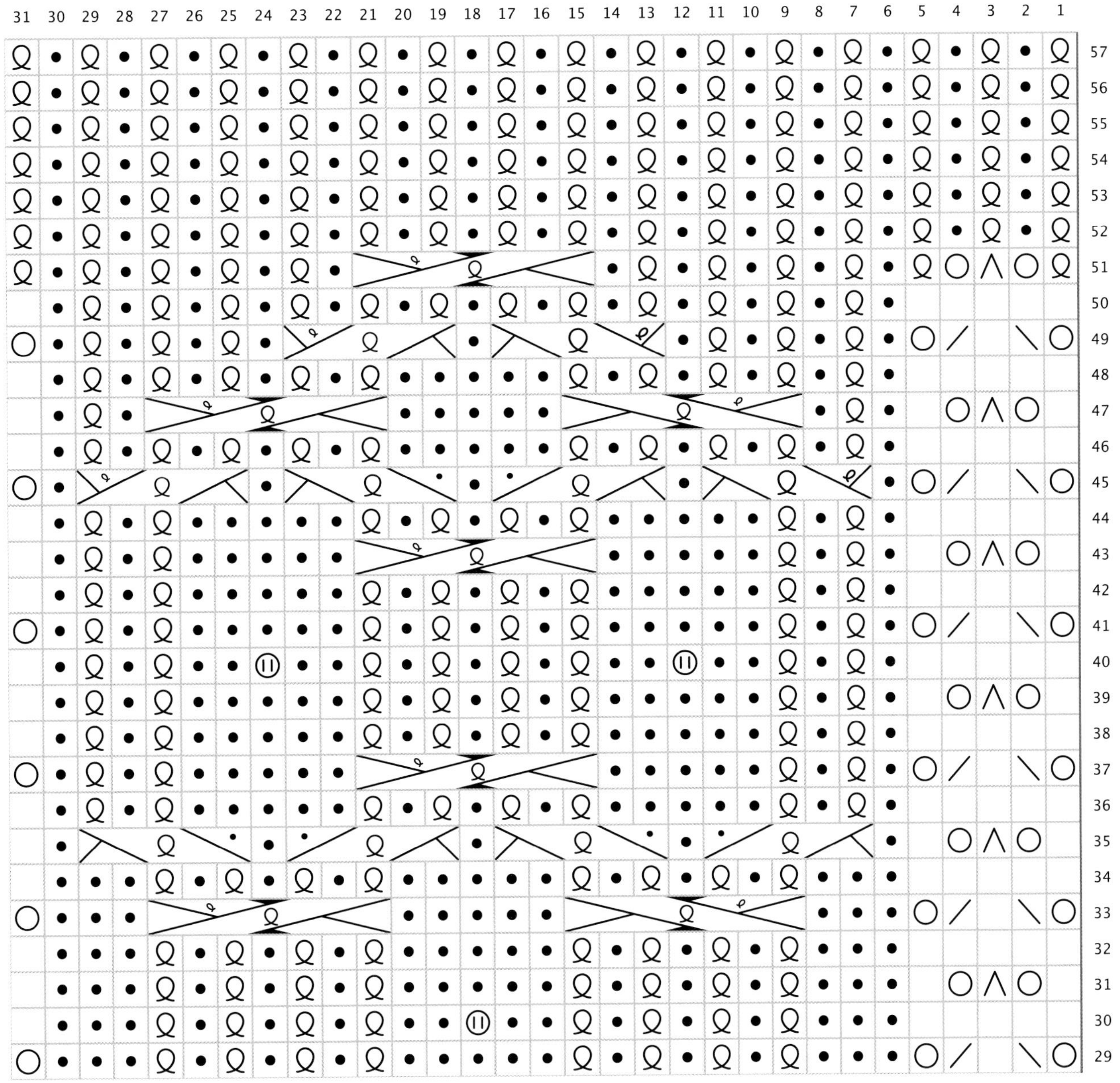

Campfire Stories Fingerless Mitts

These mitts are designed to complement the Campfire Stories Hat (page 83). The thick, dense cables create a toasty and comfy fabric, perfect for warming your hands around a campfire. This pattern is charted and includes written instructions for both the right mitt and the left mitt.

CONSTRUCTION

These fingerless mitts are worked in the round from the cuff up with twisted cables and fun little bobbles. A stretchy German twisted longtail cast-on is used, making these mitts fit a wide range of adult hand sizes, though the pattern is written in one size. The pattern is written using the Magic Loop method but DPNs can also be used. The pattern will direct you how to distribute the stitches.

SKILL LEVEL

- Complex

SIZE

- One size, for adults

FINISHED MEASUREMENTS

- 9¼ inches (23 cm) circumference x 11¾ inches (29 cm) long, blocked

MATERIALS

Yarn

- Worsted weight, Malabrigo Rios (100% superwash Merino wool), 210 yds (192 m) per 100-g skein

Yardage

- 150 yards (137 m)

Shown In

- Pearl Ten colorway (1 skein)

Any worsted weight yarn can be used for this pattern.

Needles

For mitts

- US 6 (4 mm) 32-inch (80-cm) circular needle, or size needed to obtain gauge

For thumb

- US 6 (4 mm) DPNs, or size needed to obtain gauge

For cuff

- US 4 (3.5 mm) 32-inch (80-cm) circular needle or DPNs, or two sizes down from needle you make gauge with

Notions

- 2 cable needles
- Stitch markers
- Tapestry needle
- Blocking materials

GAUGE

- 22½ sts x 19 rnds = 3 inches (7.5 cm) in 1x1 rib in the round using larger needle (blocked)

SPECIAL TECHNIQUES

- German twisted longtail cast-on (page 166)

(continued)

CABLE ABBREVIATIONS

All other abbreviations can be found on page 164.

- 3/2 RTC = 3/2 right twist cable
- 3/2 LTC = 3/2 left twist cable
- 3/2 RTPC = 3/2 right twist purl cable
- 3/2 LTPC = 3/2 left twist purl cable
- 3/1/3 RTC = 3/1/3 right twist cable
- 3/1/3 LTC = 3/1/3 left twist cable

SPECIAL STITCHES

- **3/2 RTC:** Sl next 2 sts to CN and place at back of work, k1tbl, p1, k1tbl, then p1, k1tbl from CN.
- **3/2 LTC:** Sl next 3 sts to CN and place at front of work, k1tbl, p1, then k1tbl, p1, k1tbl from CN.
- **3/2 RTPC:** Sl next 2 sts to CN and place at back of work, k1tbl, p1, k1tbl, then p2 from CN.
- **3/2 LTPC:** Sl next 3 sts to CN and place at front of work, p2, then k1tbl, p1, k1tbl from CN.
- **3/1/3 RTC:** Sl next 4 sts to CN and place at back of work, k1tbl, p1, k1tbl, sl left-most st from CN to LH needle, move CN with rem sts to front of work, p1 from LH needle, then k1tbl, p1, k1tbl from CN.
- **3/1/3 LTC:** Sl next 3 sts to CN and place at front of work, sl next st to second CN and place at back of work, k1tbl, p1, k1tbl; p1 from back CN, then k1tbl, p1, k1tbl from front CN.
- **MIL:** With the LH needle, pick up the bar between the st you knit and the one you're about to knit, bringing the needle from front to back. Next, insert the tip of the right needle purlwise into the back leg of the strand and knit as usual. [1 st increased]
- **MIR:** With the LH needle, pick up the bar between the st you knit and the one you're about to knit, bringing the needle from back to front. Next, insert the tip of the right needle knitwise into the front leg of the strand and knit as usual. [1 st increased]
- **MIP:** With the LH needle, pick up the bar between the st you knit and the one you're about to knit, bringing the needle from back to front, then purl through front loop of the strand. This creates a purl stitch. [1 st increased]

Campfire Stories Fingerless Mitts Pattern

Note: For Magic Loop, half of the sts should be on the front needle and the other half should be on the back needle. If working on 4 DPNs, needles 1 & 2 will be referenced in the pattern as the front needle and needles 3 & 4 will be referenced as the back needle.

Work both mitts the same but use the corresponding charts for the right or left mitt, and FN or BN.

CUFF

With smaller needles, CO 52 sts using German twisted longtail cast-on. Join in the round. Pm for BOR.

Work rnds 1–8 of Campfire Fingerless Mitts Chart (pages 101–107).

HAND

Note: Place 2 stitch markers for thumb gussets as directed in charts.

Using larger needles, work rnds 9–51 of Campfire Fingerless Mitts Chart.

RIBBING
Switch to smaller needle.

Work rnds 52–56 of Campfire Fingerless Mitts Chart.

BO on the RS in k1, p1 rib pattern. Do not twist the knit sts; this will keep them from being too tight.

THUMB
Use larger needle size.

Place all thumb sts from waste yarn onto DPNs.

RND 1: M1R just before the cast-on st above the thumb, pu & k1 st from the cast-on st above the thumb, m1L, p1, (k1tbl, p1) 6 times. [16 sts]

RND 2: (K1tbl, p1) 8 times.

RNDS 3 – 6: Rep rnd 2 for 4 more rnds.

BO on the RS in k1, p1 rib pattern. Do not twist the knit sts; this will keep them from being too tight.

FINISHING
Break yarn. Weave in ends and block to finished dimensions.

Campfire Stories Fingerless Mitts Chart Instructions

RIGHT MITT (FN)
RNDS 1 – 8: (K1tbl, p1) 13 times.

RND 9: (K1tbl, p1) 5 times, 3/1/3 RTC, (p1, k1tbl) 4 times, p1.

RND 10: Rep rnd 1.

RND 11: (K1tbl, p1) 4 times, 3/2 RTPC, p1, 3/2 LTPC, (p1, k1tbl) 3 times, p1.

RND 12: (K1tbl, p1) 5 times, k1tbl, p5, (k1tbl, p1) 5 times.

RND 13: (K1tbl, p1) 2 times, 3/1/3 RTC, p5, 3/1/3 LTC, p1, k1tbl, p1.

RND 14: Rep rnd 12.

RND 15: K1tbl, (p1, 3/2 RTPC, p1, 3/2 LTPC) 2 times, p1.

RND 16: *(K1tbl, p1) 2 times, k1tbl, p5, k1tbl, p1; rep from * once more, k1tbl, p1.

RND 17: (K1tbl, p1) 2 times, k1tbl, p5, 3/1/3 RTC, p5, (k1tbl, p1) 2 times.

RNDS 18 – 19: *(K1tbl, p1) 2 times, k1tbl, p5, k1tbl, p1; rep from * once more, k1tbl, p1.

RND 20: *(K1tbl, p1) 2 times, k1tbl, p2, mb, p2, k1tbl, p1; rep from * once more, k1tbl, p1.

RNDS 21 – 22: *(K1tbl, p1) 2 times, k1tbl, p5, k1tbl, p1; rep from * 2 once more, k1tbl, p1.

(continued)

RND 23: Rep rnd 17.

RND 24: Rep rnd 16.

RND 25: K1tbl, (p1, 3/2 LTPC, p1, 3/2 RTPC) 2 times, p1.

RND 26: K1tbl, p3, (k1tbl, p1) 3 times, k1tbl, p5, (k1tbl, p1) 3 times, k1tbl, p3.

RND 27: K1tbl, p3, 3/1/3 LTC, p5, 3/1/3 RTC, p3.

RNDS 28 – 29: K1tbl, p3, (k1tbl, p1) 3 times, k1tbl, p5, (k1tbl, p1) 3 times, k1tbl, p3.

RND 30: K1tbl, p3, (k1tbl, p1) 3 times, k1tbl, p2, mb, p2, (k1tbl, p1) 3 times, k1tbl, p3.

RNDS 31 – 32: K1tbl, p3, (k1tbl, p1) 3 times, k1tbl, p5, (k1tbl, p1) 3 times, k1tbl, p3.

RND 33: Rep rnd 27.

RND 34: Rep rnd 26.

RND 35: Rep rnd 15.

RND 36: Rep rnd 16.

RND 37: Rep rnd 17.

RNDS 38 – 39: *(K1tbl, p1) 2 times, k1tbl, p5, k1tbl, p1; rep from * once more, k1tbl, p1.

RND 40: Rep rnd 20.

RNDS 41 – 42: *(K1tbl, p1) 2 times, k1tbl, p5, k1tbl, p1; rep from * once more, k1tbl, p1.

RND 43: Rep rnd 17.

RND 44: Rep rnd 16.

RND 45: K1tbl, p1, 3/2 LTC, p1, 3/2 RTPC, p1, 3/2 LTPC, p1, 3/2 RTC, p1.

RND 46: Rep rnd 12.

RND 47: (K1tbl, p1) 2 times, 3/1/3 LTC, p5, 3/1/3 RTC, p1, k1tbl, p1.

RND 48: Rep rnd 12.

RND 49: (K1tbl, p1) 4 times, 3/2 LTC, p1, 3/2 RTC, (p1, k1tbl) 3 times, p1.

RND 50: Rep rnd 1.

RND 51: Rep rnd 9.

RNDS 52 – 56: (K1tbl, p1) 13 times.

RIGHT MITT (BN)
RNDS 1 – 26: (K1tbl, p1) 13 times.

RND 27: K1tbl, p1, k1tbl, pm, m1L, p1, m1L, pm, (k1tbl, p1) 11 times. [28 sts]

RND 28: K1tbl, p1, k1tbl, sm, k1tbl, p1, k1tbl, sm, (k1tbl, p1) 11 times.

RND 29: K1tbl, p1, k1tbl, sm, m1p, k1tbl, p1, k1tbl, m1p, sm, (k1tbl, p1) 11 times. [30 sts]

RND 30: K1tbl, p1, k1tbl, sm, (p1, k1tbl) 2 times, p1, sm, (k1tbl, p1) 11 times.

RND 31: K1tbl, p1, k1tbl, sm, m1L, (p1, k1tbl) 2 times, p1, m1L, sm, (k1tbl, p1) 11 times. [32 sts]

RNDS 32 – 33: K1tbl, p1, k1tbl, sm, (k1tbl, p1) 3 times, k1tbl, sm, (k1tbl, p1) 11 times.

RND 34: K1tbl, p1, k1tbl, sm, m1p, (k1tbl, p1) 3 times, k1tbl, m1p, sm, (k1tbl, p1) 11 times. [34 sts]

RDS 35 – 36: K1tbl, p1, k1tbl, sm, (p1, k1tbl) 4 times, p1, sm, (k1tbl, p1) 11 times.

RND 37: K1tbl, p1, k1tbl, sm, m1L, (p1, k1tbl) 4 times, p1, m1L, sm, (k1tbl, p1) 11 times. [36 sts]

RNDS 38 – 39: K1tbl, p1, k1tbl, sm, (k1tbl, p1) 5 times, k1tbl, sm, (k1tbl, p1) 11 times.

RND 40: K1tbl, p1, k1tbl, sm, m1p, (k1tbl, p1) 5 times, m1p, sm, (k1tbl, p1) 11 times. [38 sts]

RNDS 41 – 42: K1tbl, p1, k1tbl, sm, (p1, k1tbl) 6 times, p1, sm, (k1tbl, p1) 11 times.

RND 43: K1tbl, p1, k1tbl, remove marker, place 13 thumb sts onto waste yarn, remove second marker, CO1, (k1tbl, p1) 11 times. [26 sts]

RNDS 44 – 56: (K1tbl, p1) 13 times.

LEFT MITT (FN)

RNDS 1 – 26: (K1tbl, p1) 13 times.

RND 27: (K1tbl, p1) 10 times, k1tbl, pm, m1L, p1, m1L, pm, (k1tbl, p1) 2 times. [28 sts]

RND 28: (K1tbl, p1) 10 times, k1tbl, sm, k1tbl, p1, k1tbl, sm, (k1tbl, p1) 2 times.

RND 29: (K1tbl, p1) 10 times, k1tbl, sm, m1p, k1tbl, p1, k1tbl, m1p, sm, (k1tbl, p1) 2 times. [30 sts]

RND 30: (K1tbl, p1) 10 times, k1tbl, sm, (p1, k1tbl) 2 times, p1, sm, (k1tbl, p1) 2 times.

RND 31: (K1tbl, p1) 10 times, k1tbl, sm, m1L, (p1, k1tbl) 2 times, p1, m1L, sm, (k1tbl, p1) 2 times. [32 sts]

RNDS 32 – 33: (K1tbl, p1) 10 times, k1tbl, sm, (k1tbl, p1) 3 times, k1tbl, sm, (k1tbl, p1) 2 times.

RND 34: (K1tbl, p1) 10 times, k1tbl, sm, m1p, (k1tbl, p1) 3 times, k1tbl, m1p, sm, (k1tbl, p1) 2 times. [34 sts]

RNDS 35 – 36: (K1tbl, p1) 10 times, k1tbl, sm, (p1, k1tbl) 4 times, p1, sm, (k1tbl, p1) 2 times.

RND 37: (K1tbl, p1) 10 times, k1tbl, sm, m1L, (p1, k1tbl) 4 times, p1, m1L, sm, (k1tbl, p1) 2 times. [36 sts]

RNDS 38 – 39: (K1tbl, p1) 10 times, k1tbl, sm, (k1tbl, p1) 5 times, k1tbl, sm, (k1tbl, p1) 2 times.

RND 40: (K1tbl, p1) 10 times, k1tbl, sm, m1p, (k1tbl, p1) 5 times, k1tbl, m1p, sm, (k1tbl, p1) 2 times. [38 sts]

RNDS 41 – 42: (K1tbl, p1) 10 times, k1tbl, sm, (p1, k1tbl) 6 times, p1, sm, (k1tbl, p1) 2 times.

RND 43: (K1tbl, p1) 10 times, k1tbl, remove marker, place 13 thumb sts onto waste yarn, remove second marker, CO1, (k1tbl, p1) 2 times. (26 sts)

RNDS 44 – 56: (K1tbl, p1) 13 times.

LEFT MITT (BN)

RNDS 1 – 8: (K1tbl, p1) 13 times.

RND 9: (K1tbl, p1) 4 times, 3/1/3 LTC, (p1, k1tbl) 5 times, p1.

RND 10: Rep rnd 1.

RND 11: (K1tbl, p1) 3 times, 3/2 RTPC, p1, 3/2 LTPC, (p1, k1tbl) 4 times, p1.

RND 12: (K1tbl, p1) 4 times, k1tbl, p5, (k1tbl, p1) 6 times.

RND 13: K1tbl, p1, 3/1/3 RTC, p5, 3/1/3 LTC, (p1, k1tbl) 2 times, p1.

RND 14: Rep rnd 12.

RND 15: (3/2 RTPC, p1, 3/2 LTPC, p1) 2 times, k1tbl, p1.

(continued)

RND 16: *K1tbl, p1, k1tbl, p5, (k1tbl, p1) 2 times; rep from * once more, k1tbl, p1.

RND 17: K1tbl, p1, k1tbl, p5, 3/1/3 LTC, p5, (k1tbl, p1) 3 times.

RNDS 18 – 19: *K1tbl, p1, k1tbl, p5, (k1tbl, p1) 2 times; rep from * once more, k1tbl, p1.

RND 20: *K1tbl, p1, k1tbl, p2, mb, p2, (k1tbl, p1) 2 times; rep from * once more, k1tbl, p1.

RNDS 21 – 22: *K1tbl, p1, k1tbl, p5, (k1tbl, p1) 2 times; rep from * once more, k1tbl, p1.

RND 23: Rep rnd 17.

RND 24: Rep rnd 16.

RND 25: (3/2 LTPC, p1, 3/2 RTPC, p1) 2 times, k1tbl, p1.

RND 26: P2, (k1tbl, p1) 3 times, k1tbl, p5, (k1tbl, p1) 3 times, k1tbl, p3, k1tbl, p1.

RND 27: P2, 3/1/3 LTC, p5, 3/1/3 RTC, p3, k1tbl, p1.

RNDS 28 – 29: P2, (k1tbl, p1) 3 times, k1tbl, p5, (k1tbl, p1) 3 times, k1tbl, p3, k1tbl, p1.

RND 30: P2, (k1tbl, p1) 3 times, k1tbl, p2, mb, p2, (k1tbl, p1) 3 times, k1tbl, p3, k1tbl, p1.

RNDS 31 – 32: P2, (k1tbl, p1) 3 times, k1tbl, p5, (k1tbl, p1) 3 times, k1tbl, p3, k1tbl, p1.

RND 33: Rep rnd 27.

RND 34: Rep rnd 26.

RND 35: Rep rnd 15.

RND 36: Rep rnd 16.

RND 37: Rep rnd 17.

RNDS 38 – 39: *K1tbl, p1, k1tbl, p5, (k1tbl, p1) 2 times; rep from * once more, k1tbl, p1.

RND 40: Rep rnd 20.

RNDS 41 – 42: *K1tbl, p1, k1tbl, p5, (k1tbl, p1) 2 times; rep from * once more, k1tbl, p1.

RND 43: Rep rnd 17.

RND 44: Rep rnd 16.

RND 45: 3/2 LTC, p1, 3/2 RTPC, p1, 3/2 LTPC, p1, 3/2 RTC, p1, k1tbl, p1.

RND 46: Rep rnd 12.

RND 47: K1tbl, p1, 3/1/3 LTC, p5, 3/1/3 RTC, (p1, k1tbl) 2 times, p1.

RND 48: Rep rnd 12.

RND 49: (K1tbl, p1) 3 times, 3/2 LTC, p1, 3/2 RTC, (p1, k1tbl) 4 times, p1.

RND 50: Rep rnd 1.

RND 51: Rep rnd 9.

RNDS 52 – 56: (K1tbl, p1) 13 times.

Campfire Stories Fingerless Mitts
Schematic

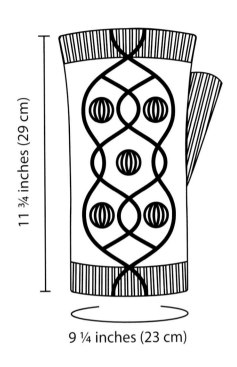

11 ¾ inches (29 cm)

9 ¼ inches (23 cm)

Campfire Stories Fingerless Mitts
Chart Key

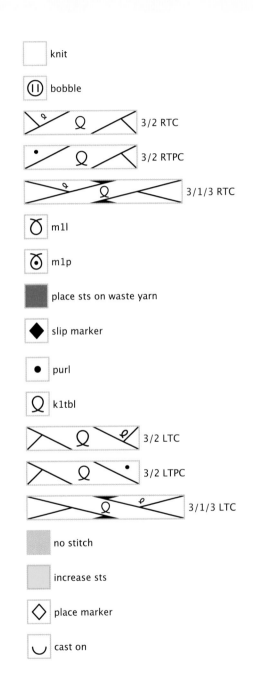

knit

bobble

3/2 RTC

3/2 RTPC

3/1/3 RTC

m1l

m1p

place sts on waste yarn

slip marker

purl

k1tbl

3/2 LTC

3/2 LTPC

3/1/3 LTC

no stitch

increase sts

place marker

cast on

Campfire Stories Fingerless Mitts Chart (Right BN Bottom)

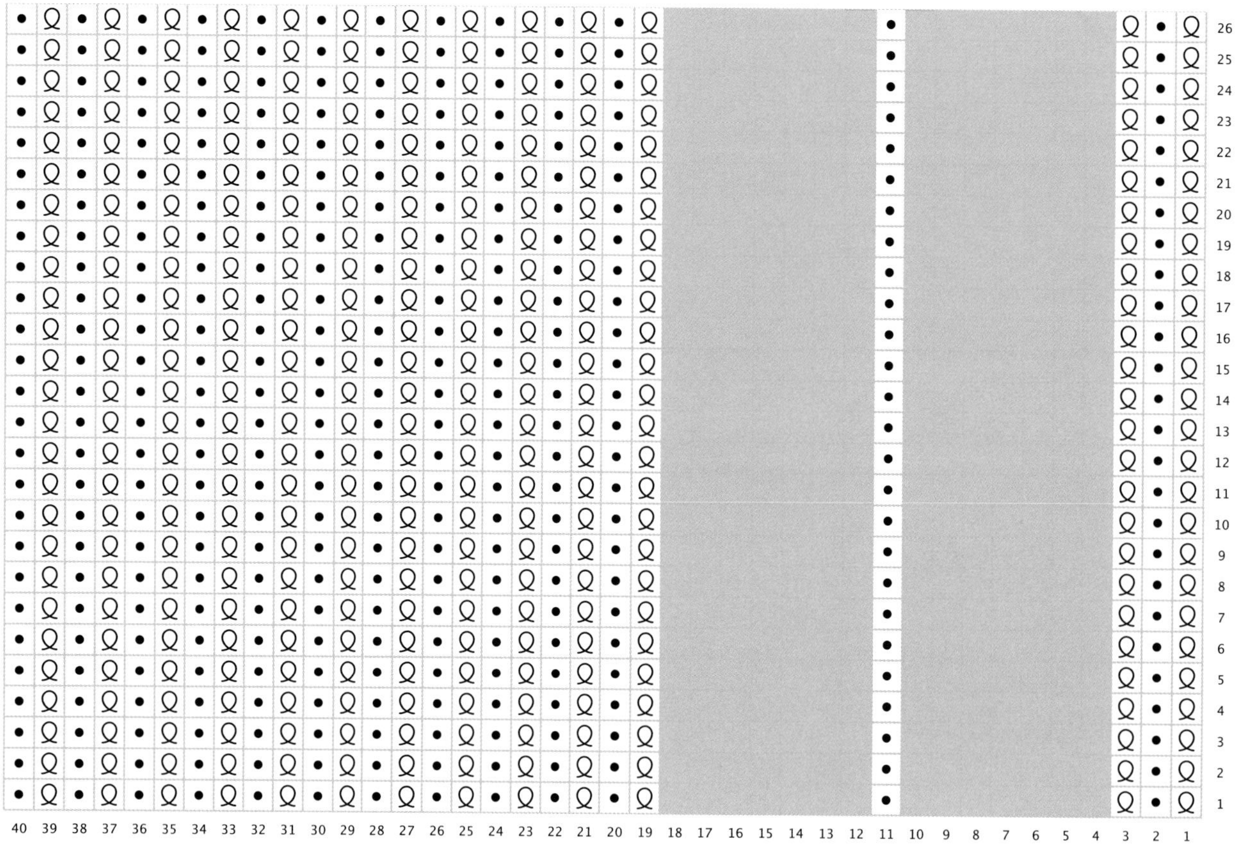

Campfire Stories Fingerless Mitts Chart (Right FN Bottom)

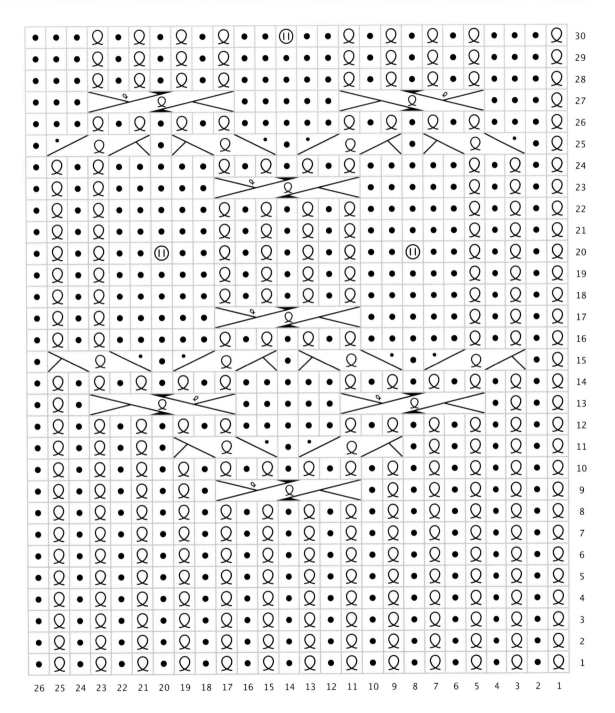

Campfire Stories Fingerless Mitts Chart (Right BN Top)

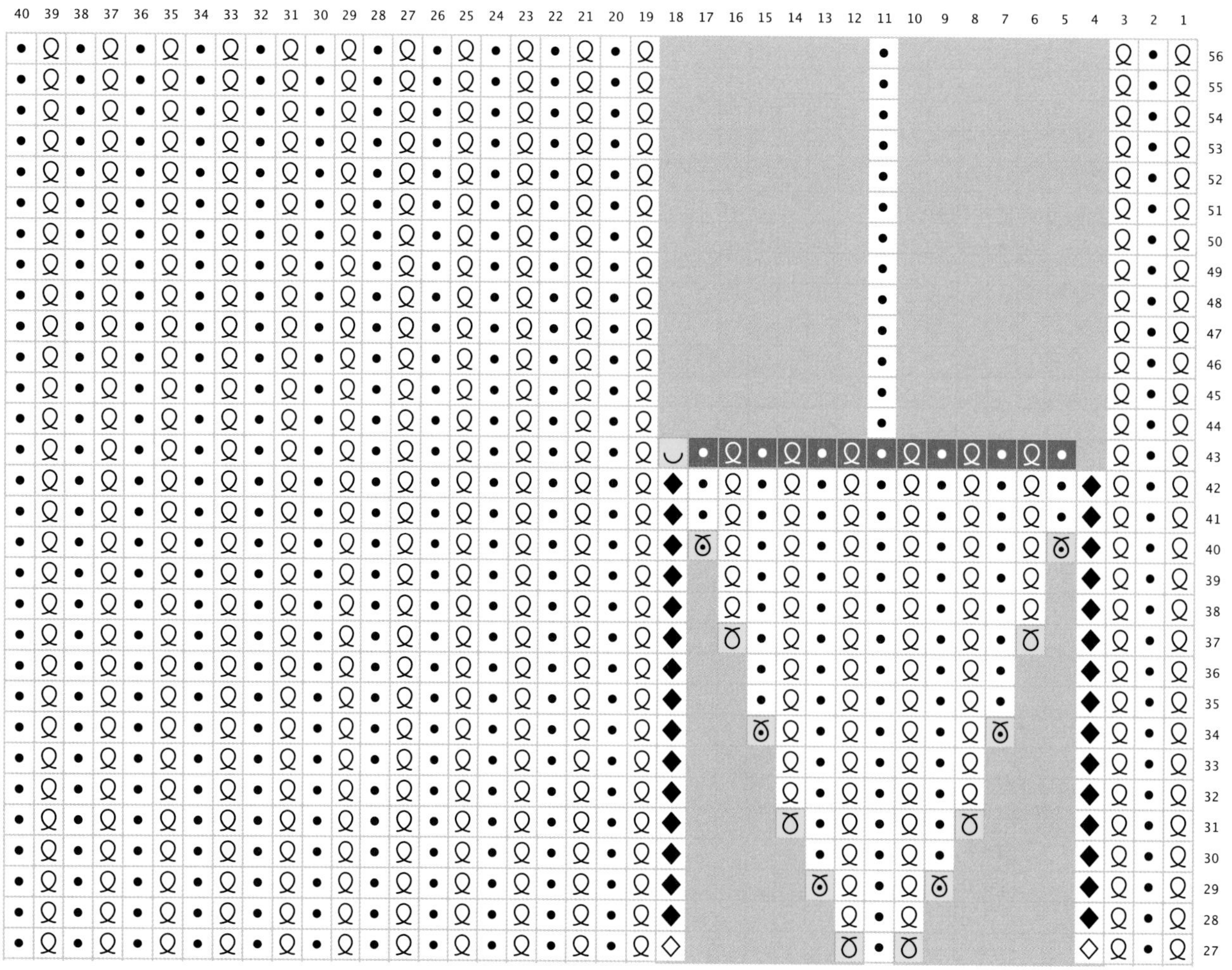

Campfire Stories Fingerless Mitts Chart (Right FN Top)

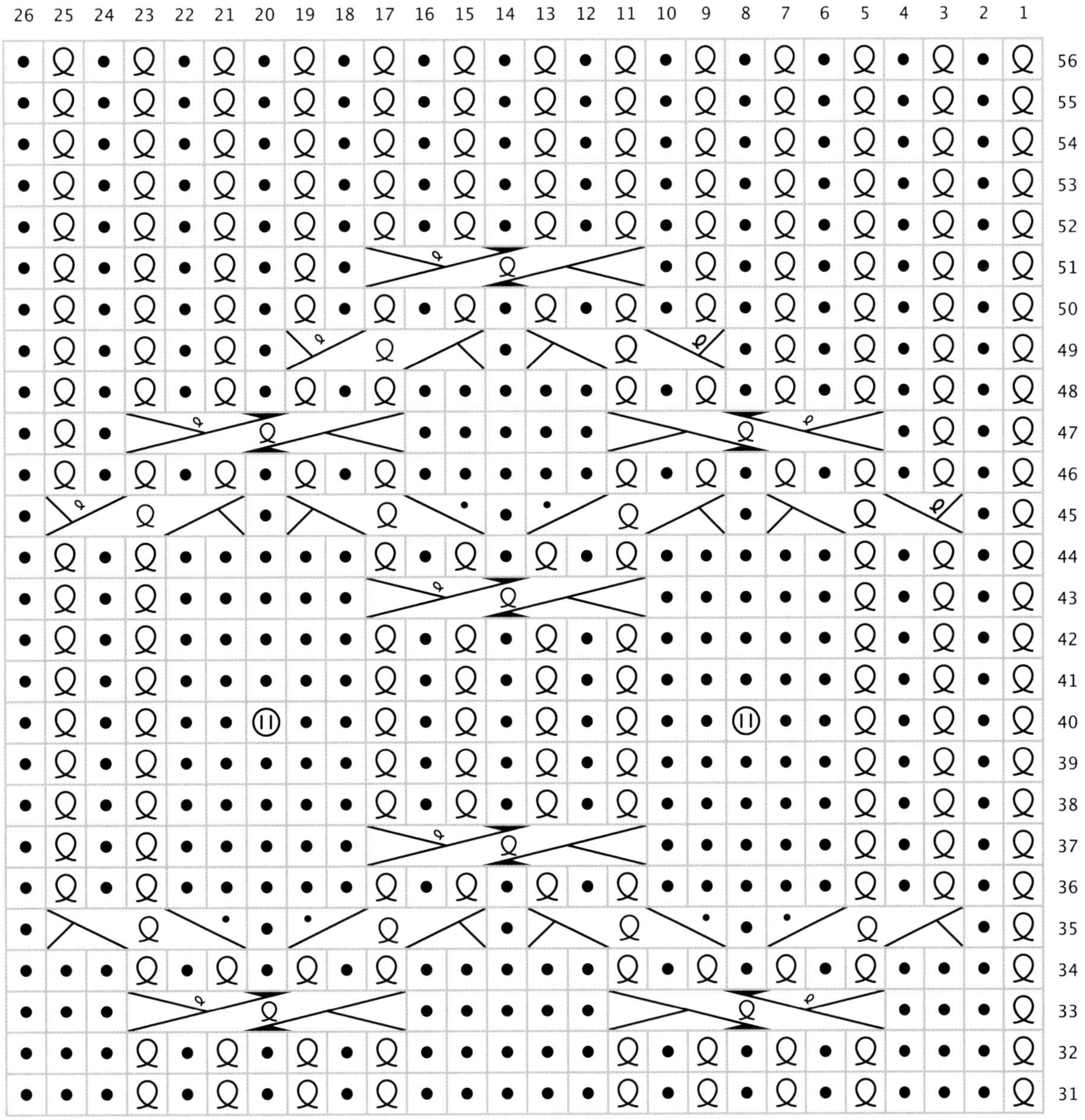

Campfire Stories Fingerless Mitts Chart (Left BN Bottom)

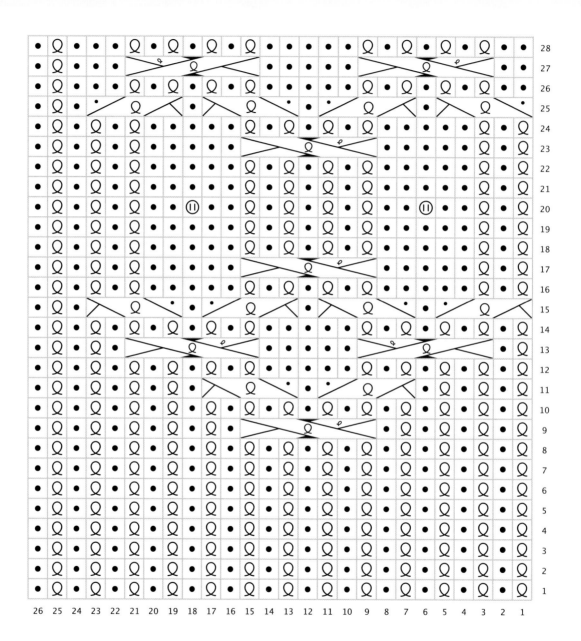

Campfire Stories Fingerless Mitts Chart (Left FN Bottom)

	40	39	38	37	36	35	34	33	32	31	30	29	28	27	26	25	24	23	22	21	20	19	18	17	16	15	14	13	12	11	10	9	8	7	6	5	4	3	2	1
26	•	Q	•	Q								•								Q	•	Q	•	Q	•	Q	•	Q	•	Q	•	Q	•	Q	•	Q	•	Q	•	Q
25	•	Q	•	Q								•								Q	•	Q	•	Q	•	Q	•	Q	•	Q	•	Q	•	Q	•	Q	•	Q	•	Q
24	•	Q	•	Q								•								Q	•	Q	•	Q	•	Q	•	Q	•	Q	•	Q	•	Q	•	Q	•	Q	•	Q
23	•	Q	•	Q								•								Q	•	Q	•	Q	•	Q	•	Q	•	Q	•	Q	•	Q	•	Q	•	Q	•	Q
22	•	Q	•	Q								•								Q	•	Q	•	Q	•	Q	•	Q	•	Q	•	Q	•	Q	•	Q	•	Q	•	Q
21	•	Q	•	Q								•								Q	•	Q	•	Q	•	Q	•	Q	•	Q	•	Q	•	Q	•	Q	•	Q	•	Q
20	•	Q	•	Q								•								Q	•	Q	•	Q	•	Q	•	Q	•	Q	•	Q	•	Q	•	Q	•	Q	•	Q
19	•	Q	•	Q								•								Q	•	Q	•	Q	•	Q	•	Q	•	Q	•	Q	•	Q	•	Q	•	Q	•	Q
18	•	Q	•	Q								•								Q	•	Q	•	Q	•	Q	•	Q	•	Q	•	Q	•	Q	•	Q	•	Q	•	Q
17	•	Q	•	Q								•								Q	•	Q	•	Q	•	Q	•	Q	•	Q	•	Q	•	Q	•	Q	•	Q	•	Q
16	•	Q	•	Q								•								Q	•	Q	•	Q	•	Q	•	Q	•	Q	•	Q	•	Q	•	Q	•	Q	•	Q
15	•	Q	•	Q								•								Q	•	Q	•	Q	•	Q	•	Q	•	Q	•	Q	•	Q	•	Q	•	Q	•	Q
14	•	Q	•	Q								•								Q	•	Q	•	Q	•	Q	•	Q	•	Q	•	Q	•	Q	•	Q	•	Q	•	Q
13	•	Q	•	Q								•								Q	•	Q	•	Q	•	Q	•	Q	•	Q	•	Q	•	Q	•	Q	•	Q	•	Q
12	•	Q	•	Q								•								Q	•	Q	•	Q	•	Q	•	Q	•	Q	•	Q	•	Q	•	Q	•	Q	•	Q
11	•	Q	•	Q								•								Q	•	Q	•	Q	•	Q	•	Q	•	Q	•	Q	•	Q	•	Q	•	Q	•	Q
10	•	Q	•	Q								•								Q	•	Q	•	Q	•	Q	•	Q	•	Q	•	Q	•	Q	•	Q	•	Q	•	Q
9	•	Q	•	Q								•								Q	•	Q	•	Q	•	Q	•	Q	•	Q	•	Q	•	Q	•	Q	•	Q	•	Q
8	•	Q	•	Q								•								Q	•	Q	•	Q	•	Q	•	Q	•	Q	•	Q	•	Q	•	Q	•	Q	•	Q
7	•	Q	•	Q								•								Q	•	Q	•	Q	•	Q	•	Q	•	Q	•	Q	•	Q	•	Q	•	Q	•	Q
6	•	Q	•	Q								•								Q	•	Q	•	Q	•	Q	•	Q	•	Q	•	Q	•	Q	•	Q	•	Q	•	Q
5	•	Q	•	Q								•								Q	•	Q	•	Q	•	Q	•	Q	•	Q	•	Q	•	Q	•	Q	•	Q	•	Q
4	•	Q	•	Q								•								Q	•	Q	•	Q	•	Q	•	Q	•	Q	•	Q	•	Q	•	Q	•	Q	•	Q
3	•	Q	•	Q								•								Q	•	Q	•	Q	•	Q	•	Q	•	Q	•	Q	•	Q	•	Q	•	Q	•	Q
2	•	Q	•	Q								•								Q	•	Q	•	Q	•	Q	•	Q	•	Q	•	Q	•	Q	•	Q	•	Q	•	Q
1	•	Q	•	Q								•								Q	•	Q	•	Q	•	Q	•	Q	•	Q	•	Q	•	Q	•	Q	•	Q	•	Q

Campfire Stories Fingerless Mitts Chart (Left BN Top)

Campfire Stories Fingerless Mitts Chart (Left FN Top)

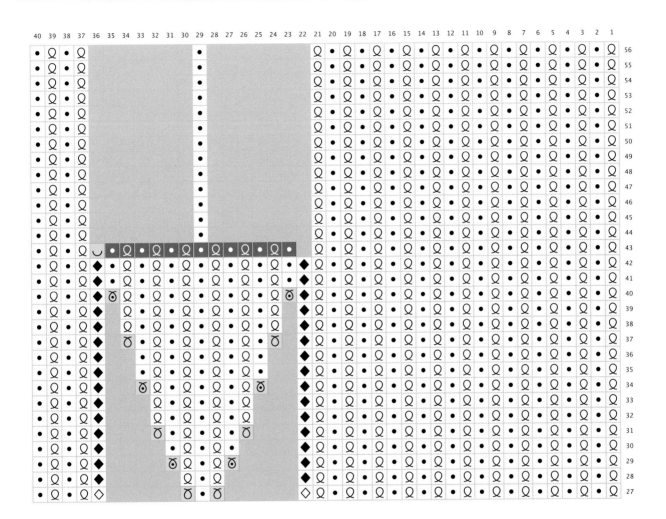

Aspens Asymmetric Shawl

The Aspens Asymmetric Shawl conjures memories of long walks through a snow-covered forest and meandering stony paths alongside the river's edge. A wide center panel shows off a beautiful and intriguing cable pattern. Two columns of simple honeycomb stitch sandwich the main cable, with long bands of slipped stitches surrounding it. The cable design slowly emerges from the narrow end of this asymmetric shawl and reveals its full beauty at the widest end. A simple rib stitch finishes off the edge. This pattern is charted and includes written instructions.

CONSTRUCTION

This shawl is worked back and forth on long circular needles, from the narrowest edge to the widest.
Note: All slipped stitches are slipped purlwise with the yarn in back.

SKILL LEVEL

Complex

SIZE

One size

FINISHED MEASUREMENTS

36 inches (91 cm) x 53 inches (135 cm) x 62 inches (157 cm) wingspan, blocked

MATERIALS

Yarn

Aran weight, Big Twist Living Yarn (100% antipilling acrylic), 199 yds (182 m) per 110-g skein

Yardage

510 yards (466 m)

Shown In

Chinchilla colorway (3 skeins)

Any Aran weight yarn can be used for this pattern.

Needles

US 8 (5 mm) 32-inch (80-cm) circular needle, or size needed to obtain gauge

Notions

Cable needle

Tapestry needle

Blocking materials

GAUGE

13 sts & 26 rows = 4 inches (10 cm) in garter st worked flat (blocked)

CABLE ABBREVIATIONS

All other abbreviations can be found on page 164.

1/1 RC = 1/1 right cable

1/1 LC = 1/1 left cable

1/1 RPC = 1/1 right purl cable

1/1 LPC = 1/1 left purl cable

2/1 RPC = 2/1 right purl cable

2/1 LPC = 2/1 left purl cable

2/2 RC = 2/2 right cable

2/2 LC = 2/2 left cable

2/2 RPC = 2/2 right purl cable

2/2 LPC = 2/2 left purl cable

(continued)

SPECIAL STITCHES

- 1/1 RC: Sl next st to CN and place at back of work, k1, then k1 from CN.
- 1/1 LC: Sl next st to CN and place at front of work, k1, then k1 from CN.
- 1/1 RPC: Sl next st to CN and place at back of work, k1, then p1 from CN.
- 1/1 LPC: Sl next st to CN and place at front of work, p1, then k1 from CN.
- 2/1 RPC: Sl next st to CN and place at back of work, k2, then p1 from CN.
- 2/1 LPC: Sl next 2 sts to CN and place at front of work, p1, then k2 from CN.
- 2/2 RC: Sl next 2 sts to CN and place at back of work, k2, then k2 from CN.
- 2/2 LC: Sl next 2 sts to CN and place at front of work, k2, then k2 from CN.
- 2/2 RPC: Sl next 2 sts to CN and place at back of work, k2, then p2 from CN.
- 2/2 LPC: Sl next 2 sts to CN and place at front of work, p2, then k2 from CN.

Aspens Asymmetric Shawl Pattern

Work Chart A (page 115) once. [36 rows]

Work Chart B (page 116) once. [50 rows]

Work Chart C (page 117) once. [30 rows]

Work Chart D (page 119) a total of 8 times. [128 rows]

Work Chart E (page 121) once. [10 rows]

Bind off on the RS in pattern.

FINISHING
Weave in all ends. Block to finished measurements.

Aspens Asymmetric Shawl Chart A Instructions

ROW 1 (RS): CO 1. [1 st]

ROW 2 (WS): Kfb. [2 sts]

ROW 3: Knit.

ROW 4: Kfb, k1. [3 sts]

ROW 5: Knit.

ROW 6: Kfb, k2. [4 sts]

ROW 7: Knit.

ROW 8: Kfb, k3. [5 sts]

ROW 9: K2, p1, k2.

ROW 10: Kfb, k4. [6 sts]

ROW 11: K2, p1, sl1p wyib, p1, k1.

ROW 12: Kfb, k1, p1, k3. [7 sts]

ROW 13: K2, p1, sl1p wyib, p2, k1.

ROW 14: Kfb, k2, p1, k3. [8 sts]

ROW 15: K2, p1, sl1p wyib, p2, k2.

ROW 16: Kfb, k3, p1, k3. [9 sts]

ROW 17: K2, p1, sl1p wyib, p2, k3.

ROW 18: Kfb, k1, p1, k2, p1, k3. [10 sts]

ROW 19: K2, p1, sl1p wyib, p2, k4.

ROW 20: Kfb, k1, p2, k2, p1, k3. [11 sts]

ROW 21: K2, p1, sl1p wyib, p2, 1/1 LC, k3.

ROW 22: Kfb, k1, p3, k2, p1, k3. [12 sts]

ROW 23: K2, p1, sl1p wyib, p2, 1/1 RC, 1/1 LC, k2.

ROW 24: Kfb, k1, p4, k2, p1, k3. [13 sts]

ROW 25: K2, p1, sl1p wyib, p2, 1/1 LC, 1/1 RC, k3.

ROW 26: Kfb, k1, p5, k2, p1, k3. [14 sts]

ROW 27: K2, p1, sl1p wyib, p2, 1/1 RC, 1/1 LC, 1/1 RC, k2.

ROW 28: Kfb, k1, p6, k2, p1, k3. [15 sts]

ROW 29: K2, p1, sl1p wyib, p2, 1/1 LC, 1/1 RC, 1/1 LC, k3.

ROW 30: Kfb, k1, p7, k2, p1, k3. [16 sts]

ROW 31: K2, p1, sl1p wyib, p2, (1/1 RC, 1/1 LC) 2 times, k2.

ROW 32: Kfb, k1, p8, k2, p1, k3. [17 sts]

ROW 33: K2, p1, sl1p wyib, p2, (1/1 LC, 1/1 RC) 2 times, p1, k2.

ROW 34: Kfb, k2, p8, k2, p1, k3. [18 sts]

ROW 35: K2, p1, sl1p wyib, p2, (1/1 RC, 1/1 LC) 2 times, p2, k2.

ROW 36: Kfb, p1, k2, p8, k2, p1, k3. [19 sts]

Aspens Asymmetric Shawl Chart B Instructions

ROW 1 (RS): K2, p1, sl1p wyib, p2, (1/1 LC, 1/1 RC) 2 times, p2, sl1p wyib, k2. [19 sts]

ROW 2 (WS): Kfb, k1, p1, k2, p8, k2, p1, k3. [20 sts]

ROW 3: K2, p1, sl1p wyib, p2, (1/1 RC, 1/1 LC) 2 times, p2, sl1p wyib, p1, k2.

ROW 4: Kfb, k2, p1, k2, p8, k2, p1, k3. [21 sts]

ROW 5: K2, p1, sl1p wyib, p2, (1/1 LC, 1/1 RC) 2 times, p2, sl1p wyib, p2, k2.

ROW 6: Kfb, (p1, k2) 2 times, p8, k2, p1, k3. [22 sts]

ROW 7: K2, p1, sl1p wyib, p2, (1/1 RC, 1/1 LC) 2 times, p2, sl1p wyib, p2, k3.

ROW 8: Kfb, k1, (p1, k2) 2 times, p8, k2, p1, k3. [23 sts]

ROW 9: K2, p1, sl1p wyib, p2, (1/1 LC, 1/1 RC) 2 times, p2, sl1p wyib, p2, k4.

ROW 10: Kfb, k1, p2, k2, p1, k2, p8, k2, p1, k3. [24 sts]

ROW 11: K2, p1, sl1p wyib, p2, (1/1 RC, 1/1 LC) 2 times, p2, sl1p wyib, p2, k5.

ROW 12: Kfb, k1, p3, k2, p1, k2, p8, k2, p1, k3. [25 sts]

ROW 13: K2, p1, sl1p wyib, p2, (1/1 LC, 1/1 RC) 2 times, p2, sl1p wyib, p2, k6.

ROW 14: Kfb, k1, p4, k2, p1, k2, p8, k2, p1, k3. [26 sts]

ROW 15: K2, p1, sl1p wyib, p2, (1/1 RC, 1/1 LC) 2 times, p2, sl1p wyib, p2, 2/2 RC, p1, k2.

ROW 16: Kfb, k2, p4, k2, p1, k2, p8, k2, p1, k3. [27 sts]

ROW 17: K2, p1, sl1p wyib, p2, (1/1 LC, 1/1 RC) 2 times, p2, sl1p wyib, p2, k4, p2, k2.

ROW 18: Kfb, k3, p4, k2, p1, k2, p8, k2, p1, k3. [28 sts]

ROW 19: K2, p1, sl1p wyib, p2, (1/1 RC, 1/1 LC) 2 times, p2, sl1p wyib, p2, 2/2 RC, p3, k2.

ROW 20: Kfb, k4, p4, k2, p1, k2, p8, k2, p1, k3. [29 sts]

ROW 21: K2, p1, sl1p wyib, p2, (1/1 LC, 1/1 RC) 2 times, p2, sl1p wyib, p2, k4, p4, k2.

ROW 22: Kfb, k5, p4, k2, p1, k2, p8, k2, p1, k3. [30 sts]

ROW 23: K2, p1, sl1p wyib, p2, (1/1 RC, 1/1 LC) 2 times, p2, sl1p wyib, p2, 2/2 RC, p5, k2.

ROW 24: Kfb, k6, p4, k2, p1, k2, p8, k2, p1, k3. [31 sts]

ROW 25: K2, p1, sl1p wyib, p2, (1/1 LC, 1/1 RC) 2 times, p2, sl1p wyib, p2, k2, 2/2 LPC, 2/2 RPC, k2.

ROW 26: Kfb, k5, (p2, k2) 2 times, p1, k2, p8, k2, p1, k3. [32 sts]

ROW 27: K2, p1, sl1p wyib, p2, (1/1 RC, 1/1 LC) 2 times, p2, sl1p wyib, p2, k2, p2, 2/2 LC, p3, k2.

ROW 28: Kfb, k4, p4, k2, p2, k2, p1, k2, p8, k2, p1, k3. [33 sts]

ROW 29: K2, p1, sl1p wyib, p2, (1/1 LC, 1/1 RC) 2 times, p2, sl1p wyib, p2, k2, 2/2 RPC, 2/2 LPC, p2, k2.

ROW 30: Kfb, k3, p2, k4, p4, k2, p1, k2, p8, k2, p1, k3. [34 sts]

ROW 31: K2, p1, sl1p wyib, p2, (1/1 RC, 1/1 LC) 2 times, p2, sl1p wyib, p2, 2/2 RC, p4, 2/2 RC, p1, k2.

ROW 32: Kfb, k2, p4, k4, p4, k2, p1, k2, p8, k2, p1, k3. [35 sts]

ROW 33: K2, p1, sl1p wyib, p2, (1/1 LC, 1/1 RC) 2 times, p2, sl1p wyib, p2, k4, p2, 2/2 RPC, 2/2 LPC, k2.

(continued)

Aspens Asymmetric Shawl (Continued)

ROW 34: Kfb, k1, p2, k4, p2, k2, p4, k2, p1, k2, p8, k2, p1, k3. [36 sts]

ROW 35: K2, p1, sl1p wyib, p2, (1/1 RC, 1/1 LC) 2 times, p2, sl1p wyib, p2, 2/2 RC, p2, k2, p4, k2, p1, k2.

ROW 36: Kfb, k2, p2, k4, p2, k2, p4, k2, p1, k2, p8, k2, p1, k3. [37 sts]

ROW 37: K2, p1, sl1p wyib, p2, (1/1 LC, 1/1 RC) 2 times, p2, sl1p wyib, p2, k4, p2, 2/2 LPC, 2/2 RPC, p2, k2.

ROW 38: Kfb, k5, p4, k4, p4, k2, p1, k2, p8, k2, p1, k3. [38 sts]

ROW 39: K2, p1, sl1p wyib, p2, (1/1 RC, 1/1 LC) 2 times, p2, sl1p wyib, p2, 2/2 RC, p4, 2/2 RC, p5, k2.

ROW 40: Kfb, p2, (k4, p4) 2 times, k2, p1, k2, p8, k2, p1, k3. [39 sts]

ROW 41: K2, p1, sl1p wyib, p2, (1/1 LC, 1/1 RC) 2 times, p2, sl1p wyib, p2, k2, (2/2 LPC, 2/2 RPC) 2 times, k2.

ROW 42: Kfb, k5, p2, k4, p4, k2, p2, k2, p1, k2, p8, k2, p1, k3. [40 sts]

ROW 43: K2, p1, sl1p wyib, p2, (1/1 RC, 1/1 LC) 2 times, p2, sl1p wyib, p2, k2, p2, 2/2 LC, p4, 2/2 LC, p3, k2.

ROW 44: Kfb, (k4, p4) 2 times, k2, p2, k2, p1, k2, p8, k2, p1, k3. [41 sts]

ROW 45: K2, p1, sl1p wyib, p2, (1/1 LC, 1/1 RC) 2 times, p2, sl1p wyib, p2, k2, (2/2 RPC, 2/2 LPC) 2 times, p2, k2.

ROW 46: Kfb, k3, p2, (k4, p4) 2 times, k2, p1, k2, p8, k2, p1, k3. [42 sts]

ROW 47: K2, p1, sl1p wyib, p2, (1/1 RC, 1/1 LC) 2 times, p2, sl1p wyib, p2, (2/2 RC, p4) 2 times, 2/2 RC, p1, k2.

ROW 48: Kfb, k2, (p4, k4) 2 times, p4, k2, p1, k2, p8, k2, p1, k3. [43 sts]

ROW 49: K2, p1, sl1p wyib, p2, (1/1 LC, 1/1 RC) 2 times, p2, sl1p wyib, p2, k4, p2, 2/2 RPC, 2/2 LPC, p2, k4, p2, k2.

ROW 50: Kfb, p1, k2, p4, k2, p2, k4, p2, k2, p4, k2, p1, k2, p8, k2, p1, k3. [44 sts]

Aspens Asymmetric Shawl Chart C Instructions

ROW 1 (RS): K2, p1, sl1p wyib, p2, (1/1 RC, 1/1 LC) 2 times, p2, sl1p wyib, p2, 2/2 RC, p2, k2, p4, k2, p2, 2/2 RC, p2, sl1p wyib, k2. [44 sts]

ROW 2 (WS): Kfb, k1, p1, k2, p4, k2, p2, k4, p2, k2, p4, k2, p1, k2, p8, k2, p1, k3. [45 sts]

ROW 3: K2, p1, sl1p wyib, p2, (1/1 LC, 1/1 RC) 2 times, p2, sl1p wyib, p2, k4, p2, 2/2 LPC, 2/2 RPC, p2, k4, p2, sl1p wyib, p1, k2.

ROW 4: Kfb, k2, p1, k2, (p4, k4) 2 times, p4, k2, p1, k2, p8, k2, p1, k3. [46 sts]

ROW 5: K2, p1, sl1p wyib, p2, (1/1 RC, 1/1 LC) 2 times, p2, sl1p wyib, p2, (2/2 RC, p4) 2 times, 2/2 RC, p2, sl1p wyib, p2, k2.

ROW 6: Kfb, (p1, k2) 2 times, (p4, k4) 2 times, p4, k2, p1, k2, p8, k2, p1, k3. [47 sts]

ROW 7: K2, p1, sl1p wyib, p2, (1/1 LC, 1/1 RC) 2 times, p2, sl1p wyib, p2, k2, (2/2 LPC, 2/2 RPC) 2 times, k2, p2, sl1p wyib, p2, k3.

ROW 8: Kfb, k1, (p1, k2) 2 times, p2, k2, p4, k4, p4, k2, p2, k2, p1, k2, p8, k2, p1, k3. [48 sts]

ROW 9: K2, p1, sl1p wyib, p2, (1/1 RC, 1/1 LC) 2 times, p2, sl1p wyib, p2, k2, p2, 2/2 LC, p4, 2/2 LC, p2, k2, p2, sl1p wyib, p2, k4.

ROW 10: Kfb, k1, p2, k2, p1, k2, p2, k2, p4, k4, p4, k2, p2, k2, p1, k2, p8, k2, p1, k3. [49 sts]

ROW 11: K2, p1, sl1p wyib, p2, (1/1 LC, 1/1 RC) 2 times, p2, sl1p wyib, p2, k2, (2/2 RPC, 2/2 LPC) 2 times, k2, p2, sl1p wyib, p2, 1/1 LC, k3.

ROW 12: Kfb, k1, p3, k2, p1, k2, (p4, k4) 2 times, p4, k2, p1, k2, p8, k2, p1, k3. [50 sts]

ROW 13: K2, p1, sl1p wyib, p2, (1/1 RC, 1/1 LC) 2 times, p2, sl1p wyib, p2, (2/2 RC, p4) 2 times, 2/2 RC, p2, sl1p wyib, p2, 1/1 RC, 1/1 LC, k2.

ROW 14: Kfb, k1, p4, k2, p1, k2, (p4, k4) 2 times, p4, k2, p1, k2, p8, k2, p1, k3. [51 sts]

ROW 15: K2, p1, sl1p wyib, p2, (1/1 LC, 1/1 RC) 2 times, p2, sl1p wyib, p2, k4, p2, 2/2 RPC, 2/2 LPC, p2, k4, p2, sl1p wyib, p2, 1/1 LC, 1/1 RC, k3.

ROW 16: Kfb, k1, p5, k2, p1, k2, p4, k2, p2, k4, p2, k2, p4, k2, p1, k2, p8, k2, p1, k3. [52 sts]

ROW 17: K2, p1, sl1p wyib, p2, (1/1 RC, 1/1 LC) 2 times, p2, sl1p wyib, p2, 2/2 RC, p2, k2, p4, k2, p2, 2/2 RC, p2, sl1p wyib, p2, 1/1 RC, 1/1 LC, 1/1 RC, k2.

ROW 18: Kfb, k1, p6, k2, p1, k2, p4, k2, p2, k4, p2, k2, p4, k2, p1, k2, p8, k2, p1, k3. [53 sts]

ROW 19: K2, p1, sl1p wyib, p2, (1/1 LC, 1/1 RC) 2 times, p2, sl1p wyib, p2, k4, p2, 2/2 LPC, 2/2 RPC, p2, k4, p2, sl1p wyib, p2, 1/1 LC, 1/1 RC, 1/1 LC, k3.

ROW 20: Kfb, k1, p7, k2, p1, k2, (p4, k4) 2 times, p4, k2, p1, k2, p8, k2, p1, k3. [54 sts]

ROW 21: K2, p1, sl1p wyib, p2, (1/1 RC, 1/1 LC) 2 times, p2, sl1p wyib, p2, (2/2 RC, p4) 2 times, 2/2 RC, p2, sl1p wyib, p2, (1/1 RC, 1/1 LC) 2 times, k2.

ROW 22: Kfb, k1, p8, k2, p1, k2, (p4, k4) 2 times, p4, k2, p1, k2, p8, k2, p1, k3. [55 sts]

ROW 23: K2, p1, sl1p wyib, p2, (1/1 LC, 1/1 RC) 2 times, p2, sl1p wyib, p2, k2, (2/2 LPC, 2/2 RPC) 2 times, k2, p2, sl1p wyib, p2, (1/1 LC, 1/1 RC) 2 times, p1, k2.

ROW 24: Kfb, k2, p8, k2, p1, k2, p2, k2, p4, k4, p4, k2, p2, k2, p1, k2, p8, k2, p1, k3. [56 sts]

ROW 25: K2, p1, sl1p wyib, p2, (1/1 RC, 1/1 LC) 2 times, p2, sl1p wyib, p2, k2, p2, 2/2 LC, p4, 2/2 LC, p2, k2, p2, sl1p wyib, p2, (1/1 RC, 1/1 LC) 2 times, k2.

ROW 26: Kfb, k3, p8, k2, p1, k2, p2, k2, p4, k4, p4, k2, p2, k2, p1, k2, p8, k2, p1, k3. [57 sts]

ROW 27: K2, p1, sl1p wyib, p2, (1/1 LC, 1/1 RC) 2 times, p2, sl1p wyib, p2, k2, (2/2 RPC, 2/2 LPC) 2 times, k2, p2, sl, p2, (1/1 LC, 1/1 RC) 2 times, p2, sl1p wyib, k2.

ROW 28: Kfb, k1, p1, k2, p8, k2, p1, k2, (p4, k4) 2 times, p4, k2, p1, k2, p8, k2, p1, k3. [58 sts]

ROW 29: K2, p1, sl1p wyib, p2, (1/1 RC, 1/1 LC) 2 times, p2, sl1p wyib, p2, (2/2 RC, p4) 2 times, 2/2 RC, p2, sl, p2, (1/1 RC, 1/1 LC) 2 times, p2, sl1p wyib, p1, k2.

ROW 30: Kfb, pm, k2, p1, k2, p8, k2, p1, k2, (p4, k4) 2 times, p4, k2, p1, k2, p8, k2, p1, k3. [59 sts]

Aspens Asymmetric Shawl Chart D Instructions (Work 8 times)

ROW 1 (RS): K2, p1, sl1p wyib, p2, (1/1 LC, 1/1 RC) 2 times, p2, sl1p wyib, p2, k4, p2, 2/2 RPC, 2/2 LPC, p2, k4, p2, sl1p wyib, p2, (1/1 LC, 1/1 RC) 2 times, p2, sl1p wyib, p2, sm, k to end of row. [59 sts]

ROW 2 (WS): Kfb, k to m, sm, k2, p1, k2, p8, k2, p1, k2, p4, k2, p2, k4, p2, k2, p4, k2, p1, k2, p8, k2, p1, k3. [60 sts]

ROW 3: K2, p1, sl1p wyib, p2, (1/1 RC, 1/1 LC) 2 times, p2, sl1p wyib, p2, 2/2 RC, p2, k2, p4, k2, p2, 2/2 RC, p2, sl1p wyib, p2, (1/1 RC, 1/1 LC) 2 times, p2, sl1p wyib, p2, sm, k to end of row.

ROW 4: Kfb, k1, k to m, sm, k2, p1, k2, p8, k2, p1, k2, p4, k2, p2, k4, p2, k2, p4, k2, p1, k2, p8, k2, p1, k3. [61 sts]

ROW 5: K2, p1, sl1p wyib, p2, (1/1 LC, 1/1 RC) 2 times, p2, sl1p wyib, p2, k4, p2, 2/2 LPC, 2/2 RPC, p2, k4, p2, sl1p wyib, p2, (1/1 LC, 1/1 RC) 2 times, p2, sl1p wyib, p2, sm, k to end of row.

(continued)

Aspens Asymmetric Shawl (Continued)

ROW 6: Kfb, k2, k to m, sm, k2, p1, k2, p8, k2, p1, k2, (p4, k4) 2 times, p4, k2, p1, k2, p8, k2, p1, k3. [62 sts]

ROW 7: K2, p1, sl1p wyib, p2, (1/1 RC, 1/1 LC) 2 times, p2, sl1p wyib, p2, (2/2 RC, p4) 2 times, 2/2 RC, p2, sl1p wyib, p2, (1/1 RC, 1/1 LC) 2 times, p2, sl1p wyib, p2, sm, k to end of row.

ROW 8: Kfb, k3, k to m, sm, k2, p1, k2, p8, k2, p1, k2, (p4, k4) 2 times, p4, k2, p1, k2, p8, k2, p1, k3. [63 sts]

ROW 9: K2, p1, sl1p wyib, p2, (1/1 LC, 1/1 RC) 2 times, p2, sl1p wyib, p2, k2, (2/2 LPC, 2/2 RPC) 2 times, k2, p2, sl1p wyib, p2, (1/1 LC, 1/1 RC) 2 times, p2, sl1p wyib, p2, sm, k to end of row.

ROW 10: Kfb, k4, k to m, sm, k2, p1, k2, p8, k2, p1, k2, p2, k2, p4, k4, p4, k2, p2, k2, p1, k2, p8, k2, p1, k3. [64 sts]

ROW 11: K2, p1, sl1p wyib, p2, (1/1 RC, 1/1 LC) 2 times, p2, sl1p wyib, p2, k2, p2, 2/2 LC, p4, 2/2 LC, p2, k2, p2, sl1p wyib, p2, (1/1 RC, 1/1 LC) 2 times, p2, sl1p wyib, p2, sm, k to end of row.

ROW 12: Kfb, k5, k to m, sm, k2, p1, k2, p8, k2, p1, k2, p2, k2, p4, k4, p4, k2, p2, k2, p1, k2, p8, k2, p1, k3. [65 sts]

ROW 13: K2, p1, sl1p wyib, p2, (1/1 LC, 1/1 RC) 2 times, p2, sl1p wyib, p2, k2, (2/2 RPC, 2/2 LPC) 2 times, k2, p2, sl1p wyib, p2, (1/1 LC, 1/1 RC) 2 times, p2, sl1p wyib, p2, sm, k to end of row.

ROW 14: Kfb, k6, k to m, sm, k2, p1, k2, p8, k2, p1, k2, (p4, k4) 2 times, p4, k2, p1, k2, p8, k2, p1, k3. [66 sts]

ROW 15: K2, p1, sl1p wyib, p2, (1/1 RC, 1/1 LC) 2 times, p2, sl1p wyib, p2, (2/2 RC, p4) 2 times, 2/2 RC, p2, sl1p wyib, p2, (1/1 RC, 1/1 LC) 2 times, p2, sl1p wyib, p2, sm, k to end of row.

ROW 16: Kfb, k7, k to m, sm, k2, p1, k2, p8, k2, p1, k2, (p4, k4) 2 times, p4, k2, p1, k2, p8, k2, p1, k3. [67 sts]

STITCH COUNT AFTER 8 REPEATS: 123 sts

Aspens Asymmetric Shawl Chart E Instructions

ROW 1 (RS): K2, p1, sl1p wyib, p2, 1/1 LC, 1/1 RPC, 1/1 LPC, 1/1 RC, p2, sl1p wyib, p1, (2/1 RPC, 2/1 LPC, p2) 2 times, 2/1 RPC, 2/1 LPC, p1, sl1p wyib, p2, 1/1 LC, 1/1 RPC, 1/1 LPC, 1/1 RC, p2, sl1p wyib, p2, sm, k to end of row. [123 sts]

ROW 2 (WS): Kfb, p1, *k2, p2; rep from * to m, sm, k2, p1, (k2, p3) 2 times, k2, p1, k1, (p2, k2) 5 times, p2, k1, p1, (k2, p3) 2 times, k2, p1, k3. [124 sts]

ROW 3: K2, p1, sl1p wyib, (p2, k3) 2 times, p2, sl1p wyib, p1, (k2, p2) 5 times, k2, p1, sl1p wyib, (p2, k3) 2 times, p2, sl1p wyib, p2, sm, *k2, p2; rep from * to last 3 sts, k2, p1.

ROW 4: Kfb, p2, *k2, p2; rep from * to m, sm, k2, p1, (k2, p3) 2 times, k2, p1, k1, (p2, k2) 5 times, p2, k1, p1, (k2, p3) 2 times, k2, p1, k3. [125 sts]

ROW 5: K2, p1, sl1p wyib, (p2, k3) 2 times, p2, sl1p wyib, p1, (k2, p2) 5 times, k2, p1, sl1p wyib, (p2, k3) 2 times, p2, sl1p wyib, p2, sm, *k2, p2; rep from * to last 4 sts, k2, p2.

ROW 6: Kfb, k1, p2, *k2, p2; rep from * to m, sm, k2, p1, (k2, p3) 2 times, k2, p1, k1, (p2, k2) 5 times, p2, k1, p1, (k2, p3) 2 times, k2, p1, k3. [126 sts]

ROW 7: K2, p1, sl1p wyib, (p2, k3) 2 times, p2, sl1p wyib, p1, (k2, p2) 5 times, k2, p1, sl1p wyib, (p2, k3) 2 times, p2, sl1p wyib, p2, sm, *k2, p2; rep from * to last 5 sts, k2, p2, k1.

ROW 8: Kfb, k2, p2, *k2, p2; rep from * to m, sm, k2, p1, (k2, p3) 2 times, k2, p1, k1, (p2, k2) 5 times, p2, k1, p1, (k2, p3) 2 times, k2, p1, k3. [127 sts]

ROW 9: K2, p1, sl1p wyib, (p2, k3) 2 times, p2, sl1p wyib, p1, (k2, p2) 5 times, k2, p1, sl1p wyib, (p2, k3) 2 times, p2, sl1p wyib, p2, sm, *k2, p2; rep from * to last 6 sts, k2, p2, k2.

ROW 10: Kfb, p1, k2, p2, *k2, p2; rep from * to m, sm, k2, p1, (k2, p3) 2 times, k2, p1, k1, (p2, k2) 5 times, p2, k1, p1, (k2, p3) 2 times, k2, p1, k3. [128 sts]

Aspens Asymmetric Shawl Schematic

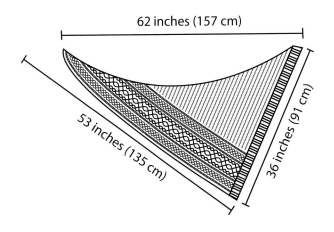

62 inches (157 cm)

53 inches (135 cm)

36 inches (91 cm)

Aspens Asymmetric Shawl Chart A

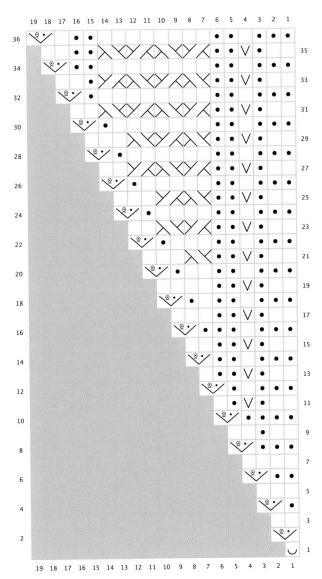

Aspens Asymmetric Shawl Chart Key

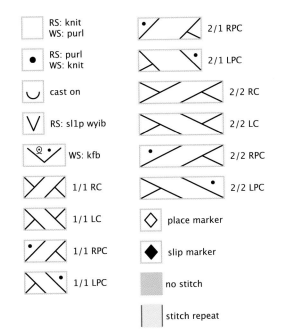

RS: knit WS: purl	
RS: purl WS: knit	
cast on	
RS: sl1p wyib	
WS: kfb	
1/1 RC	
1/1 LC	
1/1 RPC	
1/1 LPC	

2/1 RPC	
2/1 LPC	
2/2 RC	
2/2 LC	
2/2 RPC	
2/2 LPC	
place marker	
slip marker	
no stitch	
stitch repeat	

Aspens Asymmetric Shawl Chart B

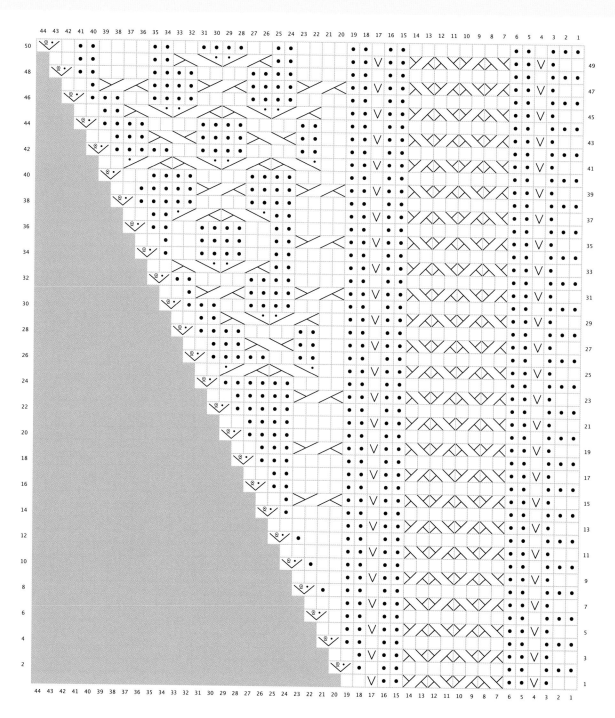

Aspens Asymmetric Shawl Chart C (Right)

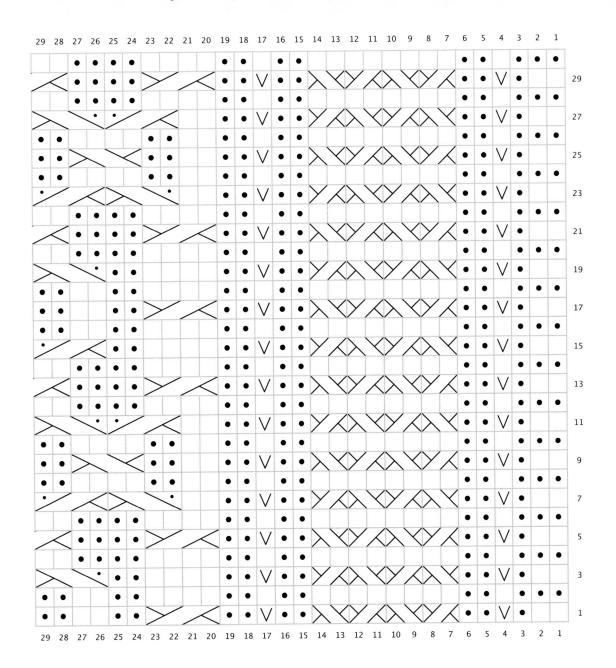

Aspens Asymmetric Shawl Chart C (Left)

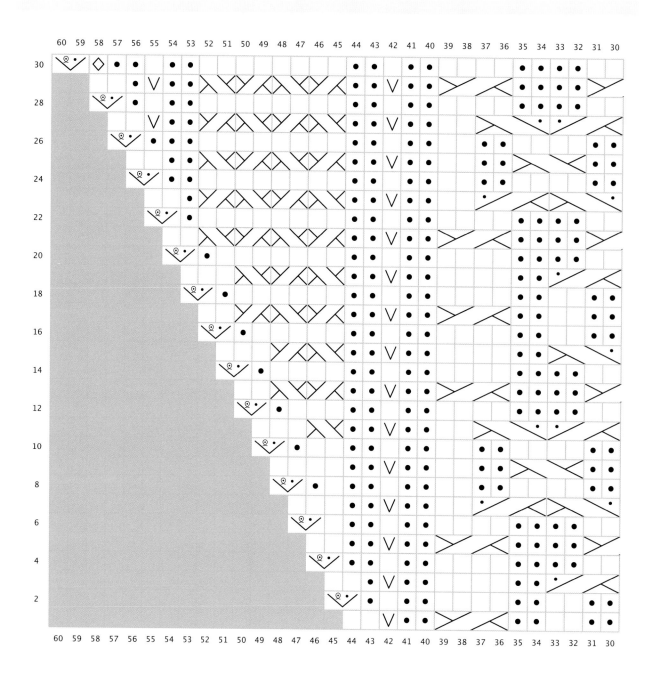

Aspens Asymmetric Shawl Chart D (Right)

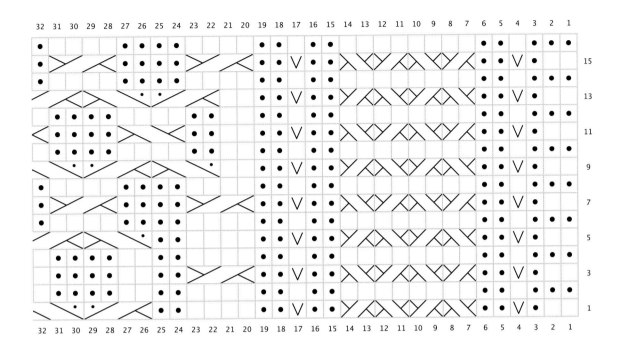

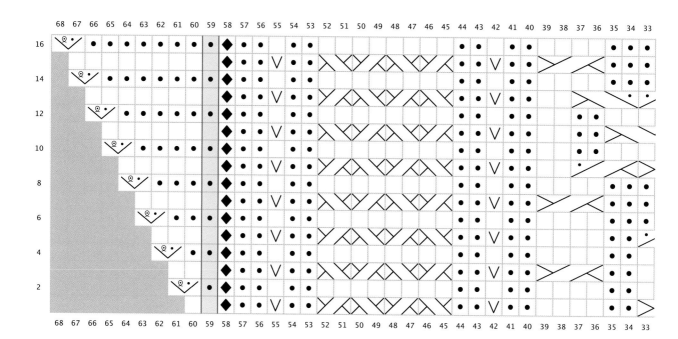

Aspens Asymmetric Shawl Chart E (Right)

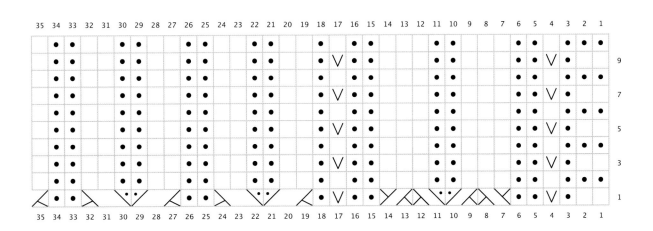

Aspens Asymmetric Shawl Chart E (Left)

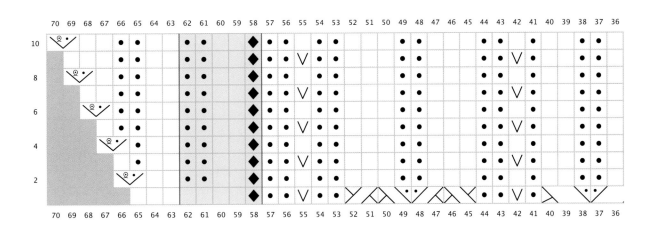

River Rock Throw

River Rock was inspired by the Umatilla River that flows through parts of Washington and Oregon. The rocky bottom is visible through the rushing river water. Stones and tangled tree limbs decorate the water's edge. Imagine cozying up beneath this throw and drifting off to the soothing sound of a nearby river.

This throw features a wide range of cable patterns from diamond moss, simple 4-stitch cables, bobbles and honeycomb stitch. Consider this a sampler stitch throw of sorts. This perfect blend of stitch patterns resets itself every 24 rows. This pattern is charted and includes written instructions.

CONSTRUCTION
This throw is worked back and forth on long circular needles.

SKILL LEVEL
- Easy

SIZE
- One size

FINISHED MEASUREMENTS
- 40 x 52 inches (102 x 132 cm), blocked

MATERIALS
Yarn
- Super bulky weight, Lion Brand Re-Spun Thick & Quick® (100% recycled polyester), 223 yds (204 m) per 340-g skein

Yardage
- 925 yards (846 m)

Shown In
- Pumice Stone (5 skeins)

Any super bulky weight yarn can be used for this pattern.

Needles
- US 15 (10 mm) 32-inch (80-cm) circular needle, or size needed to obtain gauge

Notions
- Cable needle
- Tapestry needle

GAUGE
- 20 sts & 22 rnds = 4 inches (10 cm) in honeycomb cable pattern worked flat (unblocked)

SPECIAL TECHNIQUES
- Bobbles (page 165)

CABLE ABBREVIATIONS
All other abbreviations can be found on page 164.
- 2/1 LC = 2/1 left cable
- 2/1 RC = 2/1 right cable
- 2/1 RPC = 2/1 right purl cable
- 2/1 LPC = 2/1 left purl cable
- 2/2 RC = 2/2 right cable
- 2/2 LC = 2/2 left cable
- 2/1/2 RPC = 2/1/2 right purl cable

(continued)

SPECIAL STITCHES

- **2/1 LC:** SI next 2 sts to CN and place at front of work, k1, then k2 from CN.
- **2/1 RC:** SI next 2 sts to CN and place at back of work, k2, then k1 from CN.
- **2/1 RPC:** SI next st to CN and place at back of work, k2, then p1 from CN.
- **2/1 LPC:** SI next 2 sts to CN and place at front of work, p1, then k2 from CN.
- **2/2 RC:** SI next 2 sts to CN and place at back of work, k2, then k2 from CN.
- **2/2 LC:** SI next 2 sts to CN and place at front of work, k2, then k2 from CN
- **2/1/2 RPC:** SI next 3 sts to CN and place at back of work, k2, sl left-most st from CN to LH needle, move CN with rem sts to front of work, p1 from LH needle, then k2 from CN.

River Rock Throw Pattern

CO 111 sts using a longtail cast-on.

Work rows 1–7 of River Rock Chart (pages 127–129) once.

Work rows 8–31 of River Rock Chart 7 times.

Work rows 32–37 of River Rock Chart once.

BO on the RS in rib pattern.

FINISHING
Weave in all ends. Block if desired.

River Rock Throw Chart Instructions

ROW 1 (WS): K4, p1, k2, (p4, k1) 3 times, p4, k2, p1, k2, p4, k3, p4, k2, p1, k8, p2, k1, p2, k8, p1, k2, p4, k3, p4, k2, p1, k2, (p4, k1) 3 times, p4, k2, p1, k4.

ROW 2 (RS): K3, p1, sl1p wyib, p2, (k4, p1) 3 times, k4, p2, sl1p wyib, p2, k4, p3, k4, p2, sl1p wyib, p8, k2, p1, k2, p8, sl1p wyib, p2, k4, p3, k4, p2, sl1p wyib, p2, (k4, p1) 3 times, k4, p2, sl1p wyib, p1, k3.

ROWS 3–6: Rep rows 1–2.

ROW 7: Rep row 1.

ROW 8: K3, p1, sl1p wyib, p2, 2/2 RC, p1, 2/2 LC, p1, 2/2 RC, p1, 2/2 LC, p2, sl1p wyib, p2, 2/2 RC, p1, mb, p1, 2/2 LC, p2, sl1p wyib, p8, 2/1/2 RPC, p8, sl1p wyib, p2, 2/2 RC, p1, mb, p1, 2/2 LC, p2, sl1p wyib, p2, 2/2 RC, p1, 2/2 LC, p1, 2/2 RC, p1, 2/2 LC, p2, sl1p wyib, p1, k3.

ROW 9: Rep row 1.

ROW 10: K3, p1, sl1p wyib, p2, (k4, p1) 3 times, k4, p2, sl1p wyib, p2, k4, p3, k4, p2, sl1p wyib, p7, 2/1 RPC, k1, 2/1 LPC, p7, sl1p wyib, p2, k4, p3, k4, p2, sl1p wyib, p2, (k4, p1) 3 times, k4, p2, sl1p wyib, p1, k3.

ROW 11: K4, p1, k2, (p4, k1) 3 times, p4, k2, p1, k2, p4, k3, p4, k2, p1, k7, p3, k1, p3, k7, p1, k2, p4, k3, p4, k2, p1, k2, (p4, k1) 3 times, p4, k2, p1, k4.

ROW 12: K3, p1, sl1p wyib, p2, (k4, p1) 3 times, k4, p2, sl1p wyib, p2, k4, p3, k4, p2, sl1p wyib, p6, 2/1 RC, p1, k1, p1, 2/1 LC, p6, sl1p wyib, p2, k4, p3, k4, p2, sl1p wyib, p2, (k4, p1) 3 times, k4, p2, sl1p wyib, p1, k3.

ROW 13: K4, p1, k2, (p4, k1) 3 times, p4, k2, p1, k2, p4, k3, p4, k2, p1, k6, p2, (k1, p1) 2 times, k1, p2, k6, p1, k2, p4, k3, p4, k2, p1, k2, (p4, k1) 3 times, p4, k2, p1, k4.

ROW 14: K3, p1, sl1p wyib, p2, 2/2 LC, p1, 2/2 RC, p1, 2/2 LC, p1, 2/2 RC, p2, sl1p wyib, p2, 2/2 RC, p1, mb, p1, 2/2 LC, p2, sl1p wyib, p5, 2/1 RPC, (k1, p1) 2 times, k1, 2/1 LPC, p5, sl1p wyib, p2, 2/2 RC, p1, mb, p1, 2/2 LC, p2, sl1p wyib, p2, 2/2 LC, p1, 2/2 RC, p1, 2/2 LC, p1, 2/2 RC, p2, sl1p wyib, p1, k3.

ROW 15: K4, p1, k2, (p4, k1) 3 times, p4, k2, p1, k2, p4, k3, p4, k2, p1, k5, p3, (k1, p1) 2 times, k1, p3, k5, p1, k2, p4, k3, p4, k2, p1, k2, (p4, k1) 3 times, p4, k2, p1, k4.

ROW 16: K3, p1, sl1p wyib, p2, (k4, p1) 3 times, k4, p2, sl1p wyib, p2, k4, p3, k4, p2, sl1p wyib, p4, 2/1 RC, (p1, k1) 3 times, p1, 2/1 LC, p4, sl1p wyib, p2, k4, p3, k4, p2, sl1p wyib, p2, (k4, p1) 3 times, k4, p2, sl1p wyib, p1, k3.

ROW 17: K4, p1, k2, (p4, k1) 3 times, p4, k2, p1, k2, p4, k3, p4, k2, p1, k4, p2, (k1, p1) 4 times, k1, p2, k4, p1, k2, p4, k3, p4, k2, p1, k2, (p4, k1) 3 times, p4, k2, p1, k4.

ROW 18: K3, p1, sl1p wyib, p2, (k4, p1) 3 times, k4, p2, sl1p wyib, p2, k4, p3, k4, p2, sl1p wyib, p3, 2/1 RPC, (k1, p1) 4 times, k1, 2/1 LPC, p3, sl1p wyib, p2, k4, p3, k4, p2, sl1p wyib, p2, (k4, p1) 3 times, k4, p2, sl1p wyib, p1, k3.

ROW 19: K4, p1, k2, (p4, k1) 3 times, p4, k2, p1, k2, p4, k3, p4, k2, p1, k3, p3, (k1, p1) 4 times, k1, p3, k3, p1, k2, p4, k3, p4, k2, p1, k2, (p4, k1) 3 times, p4, k2, p1, k4.

ROW 20: K3, p1, sl1p wyib, p2, 2/2 RC, p1, 2/2 LC, p1, 2/2 RC, p1, 2/2 LC, p2, sl1p wyib, p2, 2/2 RC, p1, mb, p1, 2/2 LC, p2, sl1p wyib, p3, k2, (p1, k1) 5 times, p1, k2, p3, sl1p wyib, p2, 2/2 RC, p1, mb, p1, 2/2 LC, p2, sl1p wyib, p2, 2/2 RC, p1, 2/2 LC, p1, 2/2 RC, p1, 2/2 LC, p2, sl1p wyib, p1, k3.

ROW 21: Rep row 19.

ROW 22: K3, p1, sl1p wyib, p2, (k4, p1) 3 times, k4, p2, sl1p wyib, p2, k4, p3, k4, p2, sl1p wyib, p3, 2/1 LPC, (k1, p1) 4 times, k1, 2/1 RPC, p3, sl1p wyib, p2, k4, p3, k4, p2, sl1p wyib, p2, (k4, p1) 3 times, k4, p2, sl1p wyib, p1, k3.

ROW 23: K4, p1, k2, (p4, k1) 3 times, p4, k2, p1, k2, p4, k3, p4, k2, p1, k4, p2, (k1, p1) 4 times, k1, p2, k4, p1, k2, p4, k3, p4, k2, p1, k2, (p4, k1) 3 times, p4, k2, p2, k3.

ROW 24: K3, p1, sl1p wyib, p2, (k4, p1) 3 times, k4, p2, sl1p wyib, p2, k4, p3, k4, p2, sl1p wyib, p4, 2/1 LPC, (p1, k1) 3 times, p1, 2/1 RPC, p4, sl1p wyib, p2, k4, p3, k4, p2, sl1p wyib, p2, (k4, p1) 3 times, k4, p2, sl1p wyib, p1, k3.

ROW 25: Rep row 15.

ROW 26: K3, p1, sl1p wyib, p2, 2/2 LC, p1, 2/2 RC, p1, 2/2 LC, p1, 2/2 RC, p2, sl1p wyib, p2, 2/2 RC, p1, mb, p1, 2/2 LC, p2, sl1p wyib, p5, 2/1 LPC, (k1, p1) 2 times, k1, 2/1 RPC, p5, sl1p wyib, p2, 2/2 RC, p1, mb, p1, 2/2 LC, p2, sl1p wyib, p2, 2/2 LC, p1, 2/2 RC, p1, 2/2 LC, p1, 2/2 RC, p2, sl1p wyib, p1, k3.

ROW 27: Rep row 13.

ROW 28: K3, p1, sl1p wyib, p2, (k4, p1) 3 times, k4, p2, sl1p wyib, p2, k4, p3, k4, p2, sl1p wyib, p6, 2/1 LPC, p1, k1, p1, 2/1 RPC, p6, sl1p wyib, p2, k4, p3, k4, p2, sl1p wyib, p2, (k4, p1) 3 times, k4, p2, sl1p wyib, p1, k3.

ROW 29: Rep row 11.

ROW 30: K3, p1, sl1p wyib, p2, (k4, p1) 3 times, k4, p2, sl1p wyib, p2, k4, p3, k4, p2, sl1p wyib, p7, 2/1 LPC, k1, 2/1 RPC, p7, sl1p wyib, p2, k4, p3, k4, p2, sl1p wyib, p2, (k4, p1) 3 times, k4, p2, sl1p wyib, p1, k3.

ROW 31: Rep row 1.

ROW 32: Rep row 8.

ROW 33: Rep row 1.

ROW 34: Rep row 2.

ROWS 35 – 36: Rep rows 1–2.

ROW 37: Rep row 1.

(continued)

River Rock Throw Schematic

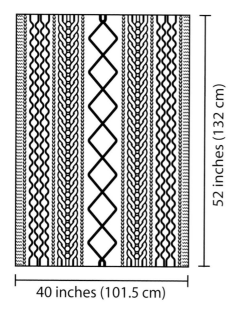

52 inches (132 cm)

40 inches (101.5 cm)

River Rock Throw Chart Key

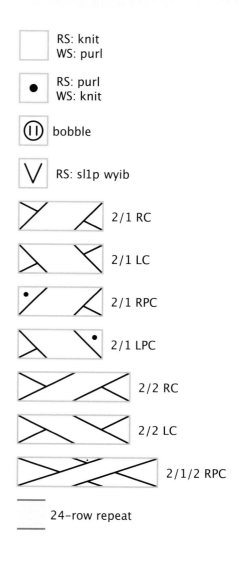

RS: knit
WS: purl

RS: purl
WS: knit

bobble

RS: sl1p wyib

2/1 RC

2/1 LC

2/1 RPC

2/1 LPC

2/2 RC

2/2 LC

2/1/2 RPC

24-row repeat

River Rock Throw Chart (Right)

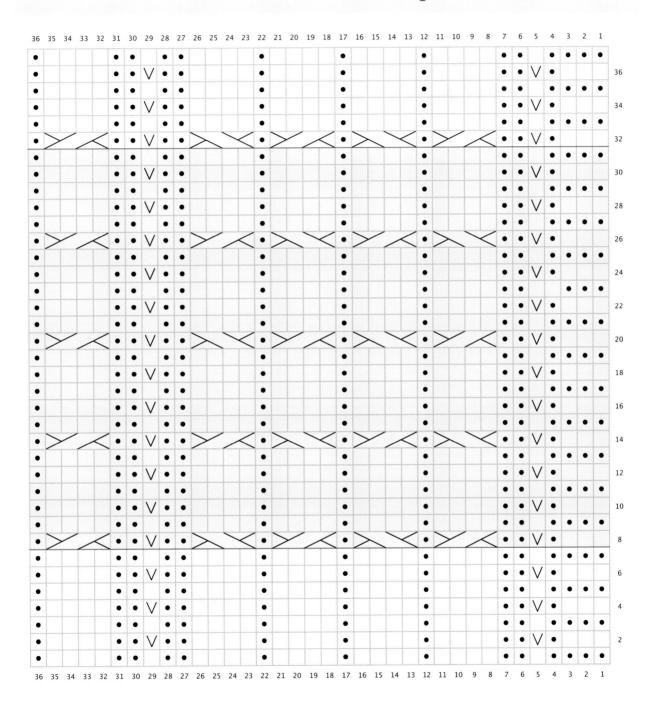

River Rock Throw Chart (Middle)

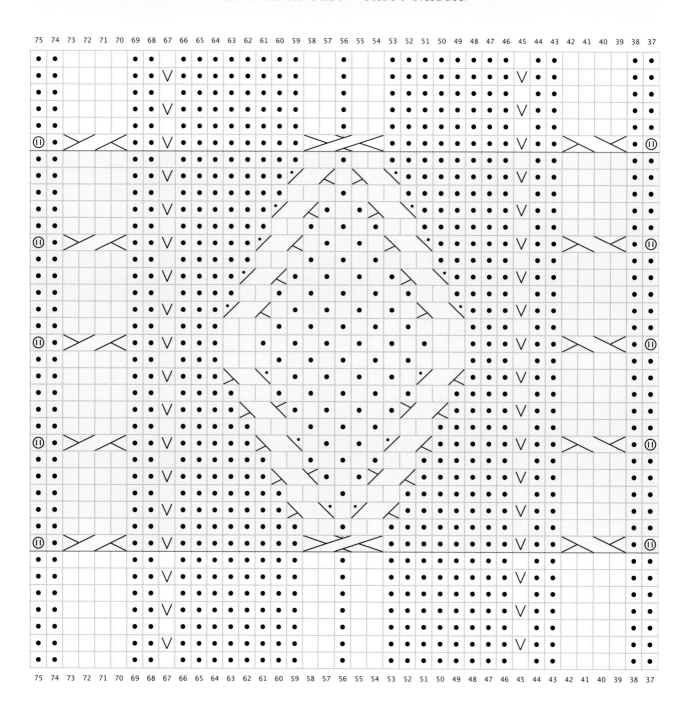

River Rock Throw Chart (Left)

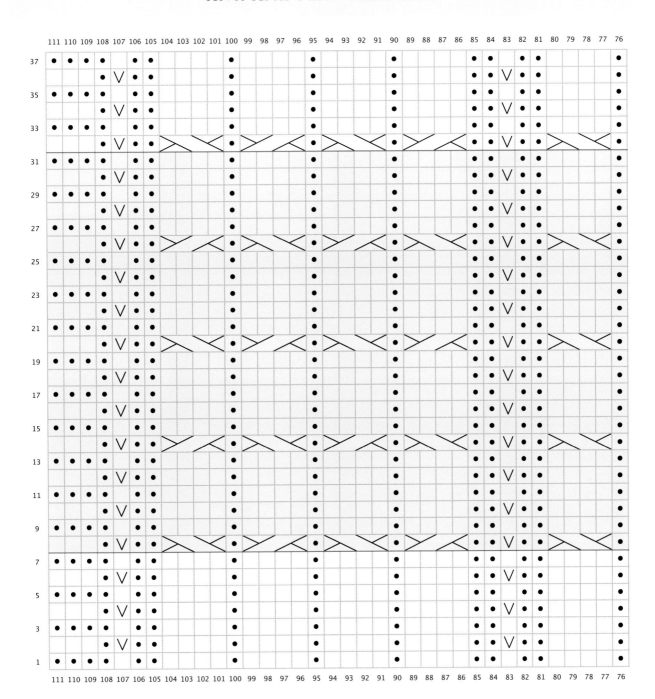

Self-Care Cables

SOMETHING SPECIAL FOR THE NUMBER ONE KNITTER IN YOUR LIFE: YOU. ENGAGING YET MEDITATIVE STITCH PATTERNS TO HELP YOU UNWIND.

I saved the best for last. Projects just for YOU. I gave this chapter a lot of thought. I want you to make something that you will love to put on again and again. Something to spoil yourself with, to wrap yourself up in or to just show off your skills and wear with pride.

This chapter will include wardrobe staples and comforting accessories that you'll reach for whenever you need a cozy hug. An oversized boat-neck pullover with soothing and meditative cables, a generously sized wrap with intricate looking cables that are deceptively simple. A fluffy hooded neck warmer with a four-plait braided cable and a luscious pair of mohair stockings, featuring a long, flowing cable with wrapped stitches. I pretty much have you covered head to toe in this chapter.

Winter Dreamer Pullover

Winter Dreamer was inspired by the final weeks of autumn, when the last of the changing leaves commence their drop to the first frost on the ground below. That transition brings chillier temperatures when another layer of warmth is needed. This perfect balance is struck in this lightweight cabled pullover.

The Winter Dreamer Pullover is a cropped, reversible boat-neck pullover that is worked in the round from the top down. Raglan increases form the yoke of the pullover. This pullover is completely reversible, so no short-row shaping is needed, making this a great contender for your first sweater project. A longtail tubular cast-on is used for the neck, lending a professional finish to the garment. However, any stretchy cast-on can be used instead. The hem is finished with a sewn tubular bind-off but feel free to use any stretchy bind-off you prefer. This pattern is charted and includes written instructions.

CONSTRUCTION

This pullover is worked in the round from the neck down. The sleeves are also knit in the round top down. The split-hem is worked back and forth. This pullover is designed with a cropped length but feel free to lengthen the torso if you'd like. However, keep in mind this will change your yarn yardage/meterage.

SKILL LEVEL

Complex

SIZE

1 (2, 3, 4, 5, 6) (7, 8, 9, 10, 11, 12)

Finished bust:

36 (40, 44, 48, 52, 56) (60, 64, 68, 72, 76, 80) inches / 91.5 (101.5, 112, 122, 132, 142) (152, 162.5, 172.5, 183, 193, 203) cm, blocked

Recommended ease:

This pullover is designed to be worn with 4 to 6 inches (10 to 15 cm) of positive ease. Choose the closest size to your actual bust measurements plus the amount of desired ease. Example: If your natural bust is 36 inches (91.5 cm) and you want 4 inches (10 cm) of positive ease, choose size 2.

Sample shown is knit in size 5.

MATERIALS

Yarn

Worsted weight, KnitPicks Swish Worsted (100% superwash Merino), 110 yds (100 m) per 50-g skein

Yardage

860 (940, 1015, 1105, 1200, 1305) (1420, 1550, 1690, 1840, 2000, 2175) yds / 786 (860, 928, 1010, 1097, 1193) (1298, 1417, 1545, 1682, 1829, 1989) m

Shown In

Squirrel Heather colorway

Any worsted weight yarn can be used for this pattern.

Needles

For body

US 6 (4 mm) 32-inch (80-cm) or 40-inch (100-cm) circular needle, or size needed to obtain gauge

For neckline

US 4 (3.5 mm) 16-inch (40-cm) or 24-inch (60-cm) circular needle, two sizes smaller than your gauge needle

(continued)

MATERIALS (CONTINUED)

For sleeves

- US 6 (4 mm) 12-inch (30-cm) circular needle or DPNs, or size needed to obtain gauge

For sleeve ribbing

- US 4 (3.5 mm) 12-inch (30-cm) circular needle, or DPNs two sizes smaller than your gauge needle

Notions

- Cable needle
- 8 stitch markers: 7 for raglan stitches + 1 unique marker for BOR
- Tapestry needle
- Blocking materials

GAUGE

- 20 sts x 25 rnds = 4 inches (10 cm) in cable pattern in the round using larger needle (blocked)
- 16 sts x 24 rnds = 4 inches (10 cm) in stockinette stitch in the round using larger needle (blocked)

SPECIAL TECHNIQUES

- Longtail tubular cast-on (page 169)
- Sewn tubular bind-off (page 170)

CABLE ABBREVIATIONS

All other abbreviations can be found on page 164.

- 1/3 LC = 1/3 left cable
- 1/3 RC = 1/3 right cable

SPECIAL STITCHES

- **1/3 LC:** Sl next st to CN and place at front of work, k3, then k1 from CN.
- **1/3 RC:** Sl next 3 sts to CN and place at back of work, k1, then k3 from CN.
- **MIL:** With the LH needle, pick up the bar between the st you knit and the one you're about to knit, bringing the needle from front to back. Next, insert the tip of the right needle purlwise into the back leg of the strand and knit as usual. [1 st increased]
- **MIR:** With the LH needle, pick up the bar between the st you knit and the one you're about to knit, bringing the needle from back to front. Next, insert the tip of the right needle knitwise into the front leg of the strand and knit as usual. [1 st increased]

Winter Dreamer Pullover Pattern

NECK

With smaller needles and the longtail tubular cast-on method, CO 110 (116, 120, 120, 120, 120) (120, 120, 130, 130, 132, 128) sts. Place a unique marker for BOR and join to work in the round.

Note: If you would prefer a sturdier neck edge, feel free to use a traditional longtail cast-on or German twisted longtail cast-on instead.

RND 1: (K1, sl1p wyif) around.

RND 2: (Sl1p wyib, p1) around.

RNDS 3 – 10: (K1, p1) around.

RND 11: Knit around.

INCREASE NECK

Switch to larger needles.

RND 12: Size-specific increases. [2 (8, 16, 24, 36, 48) (60, 72, 78, 94, 110, 128) sts increased]

SIZE 1: (K55, m1L) 2 times. [112 sts]

SIZE 2: (K14, m1L, k15, m1L) 4 times. [124 sts]

SIZE 3: (K7, m1L, k8, m1L) 8 times. [136 sts]

SIZE 4: (K5, m1L) 24 times. [144 sts]

SIZE 5: (K3, m1L, k3, m1L, k4, m1L) 12 times. [156 sts]

SIZE 6: (K2, m1L, k3, m1L) 24 times. [168 sts]

SIZE 7: (K2, m1L) 60 times. [180 sts]

SIZE 8: (K1, m1L, k2, m1L, k2, m1L) 24 times. [192 sts]

SIZE 9: (K1, m1L, k2, m1L, k2, m1L) 26 times. [208 sts]

SIZE 10: (K1, m1L, k1, m1L, k2, m1L) 31 times, k3, m1L, k3. [224 sts]

SIZE 11: (K1, m1L, k1, m1L, k1, m1L, k1, m1L, k2, m1L) 22 times. [242 sts]

SIZE 12: (K1, m1L) 128 times. [256 sts]

PLACE MARKERS

RND 13: K1 (raglan st), pm, m1L, k6 (5, 5, 5, 5, 6) (5, 6, 6, 5, 6, 5), m1R, pm, k1 (raglan st), pm, m1L, k1 (2, 0, 2, 0, 0) (1, 1, 0, 2, 1, 0), (p1, k4) a total of 9 (10, 12, 12, 14, 15) (16, 17, 19, 20, 22, 24) times, p1, k1 (2, 0, 2, 0, 0) (1, 1, 0, 2, 1, 0), m1R, pm, k1 (raglan st), pm, m1L, k6 (5, 5, 5, 5, 6) (5, 6, 6, 5, 6, 5), m1R, pm, k1 (raglan st), pm, m1L, k1 (2, 0, 2, 0, 0) (1, 1, 0, 2, 1, 0), (p1, k4) a total of 9 (10, 12, 12, 14, 15) (16, 17, 19, 20, 22, 24) times, p1, k1 (2, 0, 2, 0, 0) (1, 1, 0, 2, 1, 0), m1R. [8 sts increased]

Note: You now have 1 marker on each side of your 4 raglan sts for a total of 8 markers including the unique BOR marker.

Rnd 13 ends with 120 (132, 144, 152, 164, 176) (188, 200, 216, 232, 250, 264) sts:

8 (7, 7, 7, 7, 8) (7, 8, 8, 7, 8, 7) sts for each sleeve.

50 (57, 63, 67, 73, 78) (85, 90, 98, 107, 115, 123) sts each for front and back. [4 raglan sts]

YOKE

CHART SET-UP RND: K1, sm, k to next m, sm, k1, sm, k4 (3, 1, 3, 1, 4) (2, 4, 4, 3, 2, 1), p1, work Winter Dreamer Pullover Chart rnd 1, 4 (5, 6, 6, 7, 7) (8, 8, 9, 10, 11, 12) times, work in (k4, p1) to next m, sm, k1, sm, k to next m, sm, k1, sm, k4 (3, 1, 3, 1, 4) (2, 4, 4, 3, 2, 1), p1, work Winter Dreamer Pullover Chart rnd 1, 4 (5, 6, 6, 7, 7) (8, 8, 9, 10, 11, 12) times, work in (k4, p1) to BOR m.

RAGLAN RND 1: K1, sm, k to next m, sm, k1, sm, work cable pattern to next m, sm, k1, sm, k to next m, sm, k1, sm, work cable pattern to BOR m.

RAGLAN RND 2 (INCREASE): K1, sm, m1L, k to next m, m1R, sm, k1, sm, m1L, work cable pattern to next m, m1R, sm, k1, sm, m1L, k to next m, m1R, sm, k1, sm, m1L, work cable pattern to BOR m, m1R. [8 sts increased]

Work Raglan rnds 1–2 a total of 19 (21, 23, 26, 28, 30) (32, 34, 35, 36, 37, 38) times.

272 (300, 328, 360, 388, 416) (444, 472, 496, 520, 546, 568) sts:

46 (49, 53, 59, 63, 68) (71, 76, 78, 79, 82, 83) sts for each sleeve.

88 (99, 109, 119, 129, 138) (149, 158, 168, 179, 189, 199) sts each for front and back. [4 raglan sts]

SEPARATE SLEEVES FROM BODY

Break yarn. Transfer the first raglan st, sleeve sts, and second raglan st to waste yarn, securely knotting ends of waste yarn to hold 48 (51, 55, 61, 65, 70) (73, 78, 80, 81, 84, 85) sts for first sleeve.

Work in cable pattern to next m.

(continued)

Transfer the third raglan st, sleeve sts, and fourth rag-lan st to waste yarn, securely knotting ends of waste yarn to hold 48 (51, 55, 61, 65, 70) (73, 78, 80, 81, 84, 85) sts for second sleeve.

CO 2 (1, 1, 1, 1, 2) (1, 2, 2, 1, 1, 1) sts for underarm, work in cable pattern to end of round, CO 2 (1, 1, 1, 1, 2) (1, 2, 2, 1, 1, 1) sts for other underarm, replace BOR m, and join to continue working in the round.

[180 (200, 220, 240, 260, 280) (300, 320, 340, 360, 380, 400) sts for body]

BODY

Work cable pattern until work measures 8 inches (20 cm) from the sleeve separation.

Note: Feel free to extend the length of your body but keep in mind that this will require more yardage than the pattern states.

Switching to smaller needles, knit one round.

DIVIDE WORK FOR SPLIT HEM

RIBBING SET-UP ROW (RS): (K1, p1) 44 (49, 54, 59, 64, 69) (74, 79, 84, 89, 94, 99) times, k1.

First half of hem has 89 (99, 109, 119, 129, 139) (149, 159, 169, 179, 189, 199) sts. Leave rem sts on hold while working the split hem.

RIBBING ROW 1 (WS): Sl1p wyif, (k1, p1) 44 (49, 54, 59, 64, 69) (74, 79, 84, 89, 94, 99) times.

RIBBING ROW 2 (RS): Sl1p wyif, (p1, k1) 44 (49, 54, 59, 64, 69) (74, 79, 84, 89, 94, 99) times.

Work Ribbing rows 1–2 until hem measures 2 inches (5 cm), ending on a row 2.

Cut yarn to 6 times the width of the hem and work a sewn tubular bind-off.

With RS facing, join working yarn to the second half of hem.

RIBBING SET-UP ROW (RS): K2tog, p1, (k1, p1) 43 (48, 53, 58, 63, 68) (73, 78, 83, 88, 93, 98) times, ssk.

Second half of hem has 89 (99, 109, 119, 129, 139) (149, 159, 169, 179, 189, 199) sts.

RIBBING ROW 1 (WS): Sl1p wyif, (k1, p1) 44 (49, 54, 59, 64, 69) (74, 79, 84, 89, 94, 99) times.

RIBBING ROW 2 (RS): Sl1p wyif, (p1, k1) 44 49, 54, 59, 64, 69) (74, 79, 84, 89, 94, 99) times.

Work Ribbing rows 1–2 until hem measures 2 inches (5 cm), ending on a row 2.

Cut yarn to 6 times the width of the hem and work a sewn tubular bind-off.

SLEEVES

Transfer 48 (51, 55, 61, 65, 70) (73, 78, 80, 81, 84, 85) sleeve sts from waste yarn onto a 16-inch (40-cm) circular or DPNs in larger size.

RND 1: Pu & k2 (1, 1, 1, 1, 2) (1, 2, 2, 1, 1, 1) sts from the underarm cast-on, m1L, m1R, knit across sleeve sts, m1L, m1R, pm for BOR. [54 (56, 60, 66, 70, 76) (78, 84, 86, 86, 89, 90) sts]

SIZES 1 (2, 3, 4, 5, 6) (7, 8, 9, 10, -, 12) ONLY:

RND 2: K1, k2tog, k to last 2 sts, ssk. [2 sts decreased]

RND 2: K1, k2tog, k to end. [1 st decreased]

ALL SIZES:
52 (54, 58, 64, 68, 74) (76, 82, 84, 84, 88, 88) sts.

Knit 4 (4, 4, 2, 4, 8) (8, 2, 2, 2, 10, 10) rnds.

SLEEVE DECREASE RND: K1, k2tog, k to last
2 sts, ssk. [2 sts decreased]

[50 (52, 56, 62, 66, 72) (74, 80, 82, 82, 86, 86) sts]

Repeat the Sleeve Decrease rnd every 9 (8, 7, 6, 5, 4)
(4, 4, 4, 4, 3, 3) rnds 9 (10, 11, 14, 15, 18) (18, 21, 21, 21,
22, 22) more times. [32 (32, 34, 34, 36, 36) (38, 38,
40, 40, 42, 42) sts]

Work even to 15 inches (37.5 cm), then switch to
smaller needles.

RND 1: (K1, p1) around.

Work rnd 1 for 2 inches (5 cm).

Cut yarn to 3 times the circumference of the cuff and
work a sewn tubular bind-off.

Repeat for the second sleeve.

FINISHING
Soak and block pullover to finished dimensions. When
completely dry, unpin pullover and weave in all ends.

Winter Dreamer Pullover Chart Instructions

RND 1: *K4, p1; rep from * to the end of rnd.

RND 2: *1/3 RC, p1, 1/3 LC, p1; rep from * to the end
of rnd.

RNDS 3 – 7: *K4, p1; rep from * to the end of rnd.

RND 8: *1/3 LC, p1, 1/3 RC, p1; rep from * to the end
of rnd.

RNDS 9 – 10: *K4, p1; rep from * to the end of rnd.

Winter Dreamer Pullover Chart Key

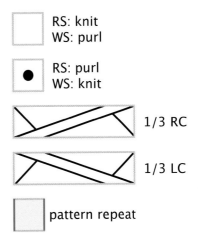

Winter Dreamer Pullover Chart

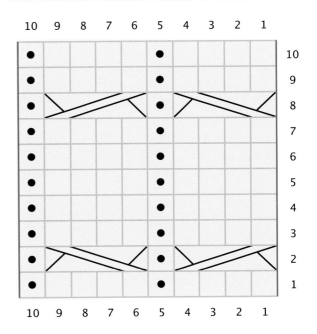

Winter Dreamer Pullover Schematic

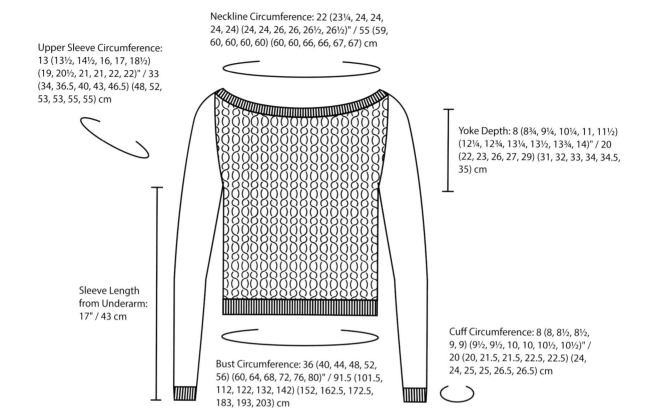

Neckline Circumference: 22 (23¼, 24, 24, 24, 24) (24, 24, 26, 26, 26½, 26½)" / 55 (59, 60, 60, 60, 60) (60, 60, 66, 66, 67, 67) cm

Upper Sleeve Circumference: 13 (13½, 14½, 16, 17, 18½) (19, 20½, 21, 21, 22, 22)" / 33 (34, 36.5, 40, 43, 46.5) (48, 52, 53, 53, 55, 55) cm

Yoke Depth: 8 (8¾, 9¼, 10¼, 11, 11½) (12¼, 12¾, 13¼, 13½, 13¾, 14)" / 20 (22, 23, 26, 27, 29) (31, 32, 33, 34, 34.5, 35) cm

Sleeve Length from Underarm: 17" / 43 cm

Cuff Circumference: 8 (8, 8½, 8½, 9, 9) (9½, 9½, 10, 10, 10½, 10½)" / 20 (20, 21.5, 21.5, 22.5, 22.5) (24, 24, 25, 25, 26.5, 26.5) cm

Bust Circumference: 36 (40, 44, 48, 52, 56) (60, 64, 68, 72, 76, 80)" / 91.5 (101.5, 112, 122, 132, 142) (152, 162.5, 172.5, 183, 193, 203) cm

Storm Flurry Wrap

While bundled up inside during a winter storm, watching the snowdrifts blow sideways outside the picture window, keep yourself safe and warm with this oversized wrap.

Storm Flurry features a wide panel of cables that travel like wind-driven snow across the wrap. Rolled stockinette edges help this wrap hug your body. With a more complex cable design, this wrap still knits up quickly with bulky yarn and straightforward construction. Repeats can be added or omitted for a longer or shorter wrap. This pattern is charted and includes written instructions.

CONSTRUCTION

- This wrap is worked back and forth from the bottom up in bulky weight yarn, on long circular needles.

SKILL LEVEL

- Intermediate

SIZE

- One size, for adults

FINISHED MEASUREMENTS

- 15 x 70 inches (38 x 178 cm), blocked

MATERIALS

Yarn

- Bulky weight, Bernat Roving (80% acrylic, 20% wool), 120 yds (109 m) per 100-g skein

Yardage

- 620 yards (567 m)

Shown In

- Rice Paper colorway (6 skeins)

Any bulky weight yarn can be used for this pattern.

Needles

- US 13 (9 mm) 32-inch (80-cm) circular needle, or size needed to obtain gauge

Notions

- Cable needle
- Tapestry needle
- Blocking materials

GAUGE

- 52 sts & 48 rows = 15 x 13¼ inches (38 x 33.5 cm) in one full cable pattern repeat, worked flat (blocked)

SPECIAL TECHNIQUE

- Bobbles (page 165)

CABLE ABBREVIATIONS

All other abbreviations can be found on page 164.

- 2/1 LPC = 2/1 left purl cable
- 2/1 RPC = 2/1 right purl cable
- 2/2 LC = 2/2 left cable
- 2/2 LPC = 2/2 left purl cable
- 2/2 RC = 2/2 right cable
- 2/2 RPC = 2/2 right purl cable

(continued)

Storm Flurry Wrap (Continued)

SPECIAL STITCHES

- **2/1 LPC:** Sl next 2 sts to CN and place at front of work, p1, then k2 from CN.
- **2/1 RPC:** Sl next st to CN and place at back of work, k2, then p1 from CN.
- **2/2 LC:** Sl next 2 sts to CN and place at front of work, k2, then k2 from CN.
- **2/2 LPC:** Sl next 2 sts to CN and place at front of work, p2, then k2 from CN.
- **2/2 RC:** Sl next 2 sts to CN and place at back of work, k2, then k2 from CN.
- **2/2 RPC:** Sl next 2 sts to CN and place at back of work, k2, then p2 from CN.

Storm Flurry Wrap Pattern

CO 52 sts using a longtail cast-on.

WRAP

Note: The Storm Flurry Chart begins on a WS row.

Work rows 1–9 of Storm Flurry Wrap Chart (pages 144–147) once. [9 rows]

Work rows 10–57 of Storm Flurry Wrap Chart 5 times. [240 rows]

Work rows 58–61 of Storm Flurry Wrap Chart once. [4 rows]

Bind off on the RS in pattern, binding off the sl sts knitwise.

FINISHING

Weave in all ends and steam block to finished measurements.

Stormy Flurry Wrap Chart Instructions

ROW 1 (WS): Sl1p wyif, p2, k2, p1, k4, p4, k3, p2, k5, p4, k5, p2, k3, p4, k4, p1, k2, p2, k1. [52 sts]

ROW 2 (RS): Sl1p wyif, k2, p2, sl1p wyib, p4, k4, p3, k2, p5, k4, p5, k2, p3, k4, p4, sl1p wyib, p2, k3.

ROW 3: Rep row 1.

ROWS 4–5: Rep rows 2–3.

ROW 6: Sl1p wyif, k2, p2, sl1p wyib, p4, k4, p3, k2, p5, 2/2 RC, p5, k2, p3, k4, p4, sl1p wyib, p2, k3.

ROW 7: Rep row 1.

ROW 8: Sl1p wyif, k2, p2, sl1p wyib, p4, 2/2 LC, p3, k2, p5, k4, p5, k2, p3, 2/2 LC, p4, sl1p wyib, p2, k3.

ROW 9: Rep row 1.

ROW 10: Sl1p wyif, k2, p2, sl1p wyib, p2, 2/2 RPC, 2/2 LPC, 2/1 RPC, p5, 2/2 RC, p5, 2/1 LPC, 2/2 RPC, 2/2 LPC, p2, sl1p wyib, p2, k3.

ROW 11: Sl1p wyif, p2, k2, p1, k2, p2, k4, (p4, k6) 2 times, p4, k4, p2, k2, p1, k2, p2, k1.

ROW 12: Sl1p wyif, k2, p2, sl1p wyib, p2, k2, p4, 2/2 RC, p4, 2/2 RPC, 2/2 LPC, p4, 2/2 RC, p4, k2, p2, sl1p wyib, p2, k3.

ROW 13: Sl1p wyif, p2, k2, p1, k2, p2, k4, p4, (k4, p2) 2 times, k4, p4, k4, p2, k2, p1, k2, p2, k1.

ROW 14: Sl1p wyif, k2, p2, sl1p wyib, p2, 2/2 LPC, 2/2 RPC, 2/1 LPC, p3, k2, p4, k2, p3, 2/1 RPC, 2/2 LPC, 2/2 RPC, p2, sl1p wyib, p2, k3.

ROW 15: Sl1p wyif, p2, k2, p1, k4, p4, (k3, p2) 2 times, k4, (p2, k3) 2 times, p4, k4, p1, k2, p2, k1.

ROW 16: Sl1p wyif, k2, p2, sl1p wyib, p4, 2/2 LC, p3, k2, p3, 2/2 LPC, 2/2 RPC, p3, k2, p3, 2/2 LC, p4, sl1p wyib, p2, k3.

(continued)

ROW 17: Rep row 1.

ROW 18: Rep row 10.

ROW 19: Rep row 11.

ROW 20: Sl1p wyif, k2, p2, sl1p wyib, p2, k2, (p4, 2/2 RC) 2 times, 2/2 LC, p4, 2/2 RC, p4, k2, p2, sl1p wyib, p2, k3.

ROW 21: Rep row 13.

ROW 22: Sl1p wyif, k2, p2, sl1p wyib, p2, 2/2 LPC, 2/2 RPC, 2/2 LPC, 2/2 RC, k4, 2/2 LC, 2/2 RPC, 2/2 LPC, 2/2 RPC, p2, sl1p wyib, p2, k3.

ROW 23: Sl1p wyif, p2, k2, p1, (k4, p4) 2 times, k8, (p4, k4) 2 times, p1, k2, p2, k1.

ROW 24: Sl1p wyif, k2, p2, sl1p wyib, (p4, 2/2 LC) 2 times, k8, (2/2 LC, p4) 2 times, sl1p wyib, p2, k3.

ROW 25: Rep row 23.

ROW 26: Sl1p wyif, k2, p2, sl1p wyib, p2, (2/2 RPC, 2/2 LPC) 2 times, k4, (2/2 RPC, 2/2 LPC) 2 times, p2, sl1p wyib, p2, k3.

ROW 27: Rep row 13.

ROW 28: Sl1p wyif, k2, p2, sl1p wyib, p2, k2, p4, 2/2 RC, p4, 2/2 LPC, 2/2 RPC, p4, 2/2 RC, p4, k2, p2, sl1p wyib, p2, k3.

ROW 29: Rep row 11.

ROW 30: Sl1p wyif, k2, p2, sl1p wyib, p2, 2/2 LPC, 2/2 RPC, 2/1 LPC, p5, 2/2 RC, p5, 2/1 RPC, 2/2 LPC, 2/2 RPC, p2, sl1p wyib, p2, k3.

ROW 31: Rep row 1.

ROW 32: Sl1p wyif, k2, p2, sl1p wyib, p4, 2/2 LC, p3, k2, p2, mb, p2, k4, p2, mb, p2, k2, p3, 2/2 LC, p4, sl1p wyib, p2, k3.

ROW 33: Rep row 1.

ROW 34: Rep row 10.

ROW 35: Rep row 11.

ROW 36: Rep row 20.

ROW 37: Rep row 13.

ROW 38: Rep row 22.

ROW 39: Rep row 23.

ROW 40: Rep row 24.

ROW 41: Rep row 23.

ROW 42: Rep row 26.

ROW 43: Rep row 13.

ROW 44: Rep row 28.

ROW 45: Rep row 11.

ROW 46: Rep row 30.

ROW 47: Rep row 1.

ROW 48: Sl1p wyif, k2, p2, sl1p wyib, p4, 2/2 LC, p3, k2, p3, 2/2 RPC, 2/2 LPC, p3, k2, p3, 2/2 LC, p4, sl1p wyib, p2, k3.

ROW 49: Rep row 15.

ROW 50: Sl1p wyif, k2, p2, sl1p wyib, p2, 2/2 RPC, 2/2 LPC, 2/1 RPC, p3, k2, p4, k2, p3, 2/1 LPC, 2/2 RPC, 2/2 LPC, p2, sl1p wyib, p2, k3.

ROW 51: Rep row 13.

ROW 52: Rep row 28.

ROW 53: Rep row 11.

ROW 54: Rep row 30.

ROW 55: Rep row 1.

ROW 56: Rep row 8.

ROW 57: Rep row 1.

ROW 58: Rep row 6.

ROW 59: Rep row 1.

ROW 60: Rep row 2.

ROW 61: Rep row 1.

Storm Flurry Wrap Schematic

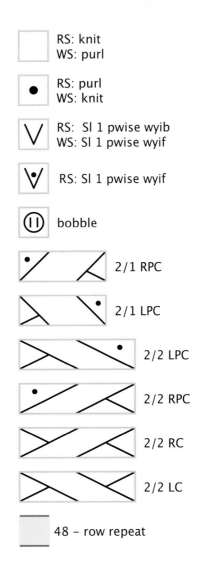

70 inches (178 cm)

15 inches (38 cm)

Storm Flurry Wrap Chart Key

☐	RS: knit WS: purl
●	RS: purl WS: knit
V	RS: Sl 1 pwise wyib WS: Sl 1 pwise wyif
V̇	RS: Sl 1 pwise wyif
⦇‖⦈	bobble

2/1 RPC

2/1 LPC

2/2 LPC

2/2 RPC

2/2 RC

2/2 LC

48 – row repeat

Storm Flurry Wrap Chart (Bottom Left)

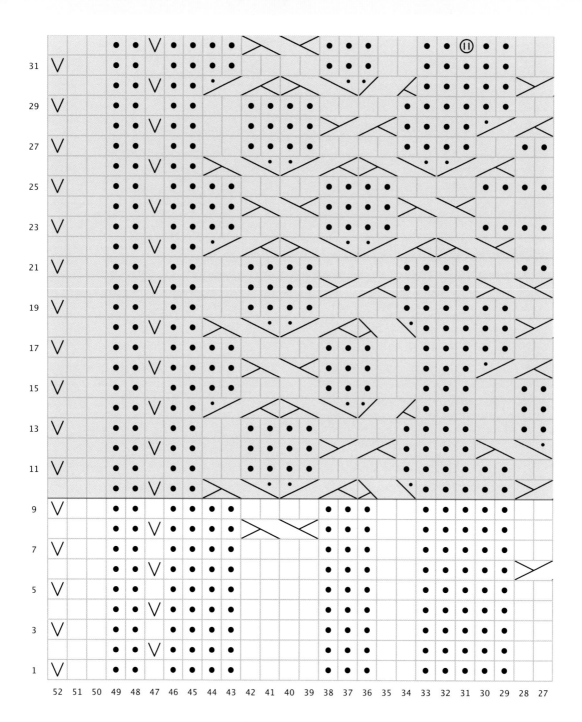

Storm Flurry Wrap Chart (Bottom Right)

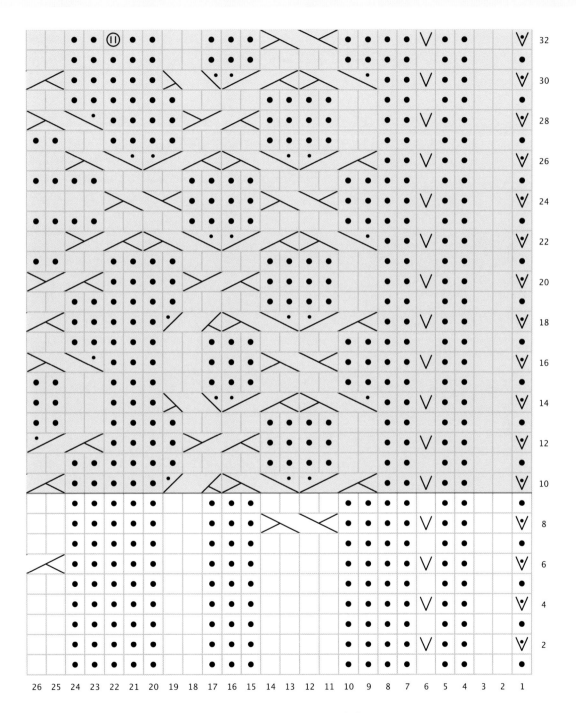

Storm Flurry Wrap Chart (Top Left)

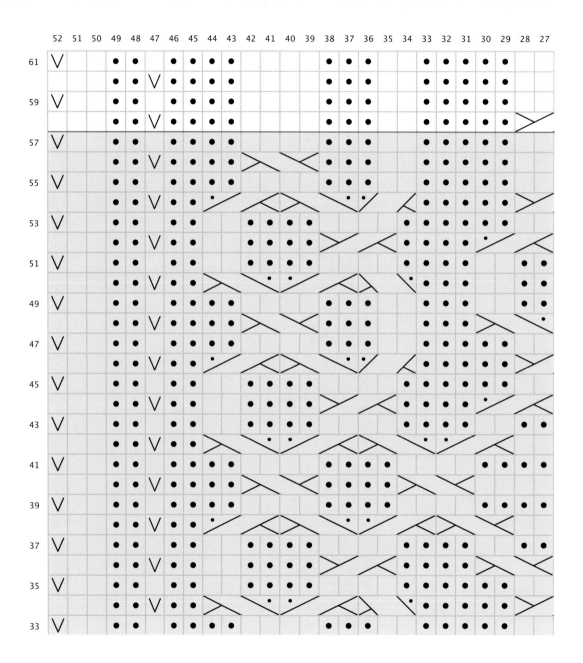

Storm Flurry Wrap Chart (Top Right)

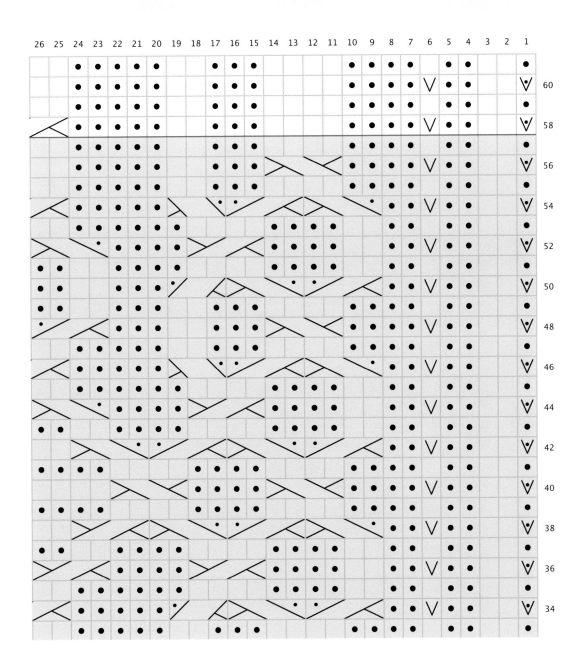

Kindling Stockings

Like kindling for a fire, these stockings will warm you up from your toes to your lap. Worked by holding worsted weight with lace weight mohair, these are the perfect project for spoiling yourself. Who needs an afghan when you can wear these soft and beautiful stockings by the fire? This pattern is charted and includes written instructions for both feet.

CONSTRUCTION

These stockings are worked in the round from the toe up. Judy's Magic Cast-on begins these stockings and shadow wrap short-rows make up the heel. This pattern is written using the Magic Loop method but DPNs can also be used. The pattern will direct you on how to distribute the stitches. Written in one adult size, additional stockinette stitches can be added for extra width. The footbed is adjustable from a women's size 8 to 10. A basic formula is supplied for working the leg increases but feel free to work these without them.

SKILL LEVEL

- Complex

SIZE

- US women's size 8–10.

FINISHED MEASUREMENTS

Finished circumference

- 7 inches (18 cm), blocked

Finished length

- 36 inches (91 cm), blocked

Leg & thigh circumference is adjustable.

Foot length is adjustable.

MATERIALS

Yarn

- Worsted weight, Universal Uptown Worsted (100% anti-pilling acrylic), 180 yds (165 m) per 100-g skein
- Lace weight, KnitPicks Aloft (72% super kid mohair, 28% silk), 260 yds (238 m) per 25-g skein

Note: Both yarns are used in this pattern and are held together throughout.

Yardage

- 500 yards (457 m) of each yarn

Shown In

- Worsted—353 Donahue (2 skeins)
- Lace—Silver (2 skeins)

Any worsted weight and lace weight yarns can be used for this pattern.

Needles

For stocking

- US 8 (5.5 mm) 32-inch (80-cm) circular needle, or size needed to obtain gauge

For toe

- US 6 (4.5 mm) 32-inch (80-cm) circular needle, or two sizes smaller than the size needed to obtain gauge

Notions

- 2 cable needles
- Tapestry needle
- Blocking materials

(continued)

GAUGE

- 20 sts & 20 rows = 4 inches (10 cm) in cable pattern worked flat using larger needle (blocked)
- 16 sts & 20 rows = 4 inches (10 cm) in stockinette stitch worked flat using larger needle (blocked)

SPECIAL TECHNIQUES

- Jeny's Surprisingly Stretchy Bind-off (page 167)
- Judy's Magic Cast-on (page 167)
- Shadow wrap knit (page 171)
- Shadow wrap purl (page 171)
- Twin stitch (page 171)
- Triplet stitch (page 171)

CABLE ABBREVIATIONS

All other abbreviations can be found on page 164.

- 2/2/2 RPC = 2/2/2 right purl cable
- 2/2/2 LPC = 2/2/2 left purl cable
- 2/2 LC = 2/2 left cable
- 2/2 LPC = 2/2 left purl cable
- 2/2 RC = 2/2 right cable
- 2/2 RPC = 2/2 right purl cable
- 6 WC = 6-stitch wrapped cable

SPECIAL STITCHES

- **2/2/2 RPC:** Sl next 4 sts to CN and place at back of work, k2, sl 2 left-most sts from CN to LH needle, move CN with rem sts to front of work, p2 from LH needle, then k2 from CN.
- **2/2/2 LPC:** Sl next 2 sts to CN and place at front of work, sl next 2 sts to second CN and place at back of work, k2, p2 from back CN, then k2 from front CN.
- **2/2 LC:** Sl next 2 sts to CN and place at front of work, k2, then k2 from CN.
- **2/2 LPC:** Sl next 2 sts to CN and place at front of work, p2, then k2 from CN.

- **2/2 RC:** Sl next 2 sts to CN and place at back of work, k2, then k2 from CN.
- **2/2 RPC:** Sl next 2 sts to CN and place at back of work, k2, then p2 from CN.
- **6 WC:** Sl 6 sts to CN, wrap working yarn around the bottom of the CN, bringing the yarn from the back and coming to the front and around the back again, wrapping a total of 3 times. Sl all 6 sts back onto the RH needle, leaving them unworked. After the final wrap, working yarn should be coming from the left side of the needle; bring the yarn forward and work the next st in pattern. [1 purl st] This will anchor your wraps.
- **M1L:** With the LH needle, pick up the bar between the st you knit and the one you're about to knit, bringing the needle from front to back. Next, insert the tip of the right needle purlwise into the back leg of the strand and knit as usual. [1 st increased]
- **M1R:** With the LH needle, pick up the bar between the st you knit and the one you're about to knit, bringing the needle from back to front. Next, insert the tip of the right needle knitwise into the front leg of the strand and knit as usual. [1 st increased]

Kindling Stockings Pattern (Make Two)

Note: For Magic Loop, half of the sts should be on the front needle and the other half should be on the back needle. If working on 4 DPNs, needles 1 & 2 will be referenced in the pattern as the front needle and needles 3 & 4 will be referenced as the back needle.

TOE

With smaller needles, CO 12 sts using Judy's Magic Cast-on. Join in the round.

RND 1: Knit.

RND 2: (K1, m1R, k to last st on needle, m1L, K1) 2 times. [4 sts increased]

Work rnds 1–2 until you have 36 sts on your needles.

Knit one rnd.

FOOT

Note: Work both socks the same but use the corresponding charts (page 154) for the right and left sock.

The front needle (or DPNs 1 & 2) will hold sts for the instep (charted). The back needle (or DPNs 3 & 4) will hold sole sts. The sole sts are uncharted and will always be worked in stockinette stitch.

Using larger needles, and following the correct chart for right or left, work until stocking measures 2 inches (5 cm) shorter than actual foot length. Make a note of which chart row you end on, so that you can begin again on the correct row.

HEEL

Note: Work heel on back needle (or DPNs 3 & 4) only.

SHORT ROW 1 (RS): K17, swk, turn.

SHORT ROW 2 (WS): P16, swp, turn.

SHORT ROW 3: K15, swk, turn.

SHORT ROW 4: P14, swp, turn.

SHORT ROW 5: K13, swk, turn.

SHORT ROW 6: P12, swp, turn.

SHORT ROW 7: K11, swk, turn.

SHORT ROW 8: P10, swp, turn.

SHORT ROW 9: K9, swk, turn.

SHORT ROW 10: P8, swp, turn.

SHORT ROW 11: K7, swk, turn.

SHORT ROW 12: P6, swp, turn.

There will be 6 unworked sts in the middle with 6 shadow wraps (twin sts) on each side. [18 sts]

SHORT ROW 13: K6, k twin st as 1 st, swk twin st, turn.

SHORT ROW 14: P7, p twin st as 1 st, swp twin st, turn.

SHORT ROW 15: K8, k triplet st as 1 st, swk twin st, turn.

SHORT ROW 16: P9, p triplet st as 1 st, swp twin st, turn.

SHORT ROW 17: K10, k triplet st as 1 st swk twin st, turn.

SHORT ROW 18: P11, p triplet st as 1 st, swp twin st, turn.

SHORT ROW 19: K12, k triplet st as 1 st swk twin st, turn.

SHORT ROW 20: P13, p triplet st as 1 st, swp twin st, turn.

SHORT ROW 21: K14, k triplet st as 1 st swk twin st, turn.

SHORT ROW 22: P15, p triplet st as 1 st, swp twin st, turn.

SHORT ROW 23: K16, k triplet as 1 st. Do not turn.

Note: The shadow wrap left at the beginning of the final short row will be worked as 1 st on the next round of stocking.

(continued)

LEG

Begin working in the round again, continuing with your chart where you ended before the heel. Work for another 25 rnds.

You will now begin increasing the leg on the BN sts only.

Note: You may find it helpful to switch to a short circular needle to work sts in the round as your st count increases. If you do this, mark the BN sts with a stitch marker on each side.

FORMULA FOR LEG INCREASES

Measure the largest part of your calf, always rounding down to the nearest inch (2.5 cm): ___ = (A)

Subtract 10 inches (25 cm) from A: ___ = (B)

Note: If your calf measurement is less than 10 inches (25 cm), increases are not needed.

Multiply B by 2: ___ = (C).

Divide 60 by C: ___ = (D).

Increase every ___ (D) rnds.

INCREASE RND: FN: Work Kindling Stockings Chart. BN: K1, m1L, k to last st on needle, m1R, K1. [2 sts increased]

Work increase rnd every (D) rnds (C) times. [60 rnds]

Work even until Kindling Stockings Chart rep has been worked a total of 4 times for the entire stocking, then work the final 3 rnds of the chart. (The stocking should measure 28 inches [70 cm] from CO.)

THIGH RIBBING

Switch to the smaller needle size.

RIBBING RND: (P2, k2) to end of rnd.

Work Ribbing rnd for 8 inches (20 cm).

Bind off on the RS using Jeny's Surprisingly Stretchy Bind-off.

FINISHING

Weave in all ends and steam block to finished dimensions.

Kindling Stockings (Right Foot) Chart Instructions

RNDS 1 – 2: (P2, k2) 4 times, p2. (18 sts)

RND 3: P2, k2, p2, 2/2/2 LPC, p2, k2, p2.

RND 4: Rep rnd 1.

RND 5: P2, k2, 2/2 RC, p2, 2/2 LC, k2, p2.

RND 6: (P2, k6) 2 times, p2.

RND 7: P2, 2/2 RPC, k2, p2, k2, 2/2 LPC, p2.

RNDS 8 – 9: Rep rnd 1.

RNDS 10 – 15: Rep rnds 4–9.

RND 16: Rep rnd 1.

RND 17: P2, k2, p2, 6 WC, p2, k2, p2.

RNDS 18 – 20: (P2, k2) 4 times, p2.

RND 21: P2, 2/2 LC, k2, p2, k2, 2/2 RC, p2.

RND 22: Rep rnd 6.

RND 23: P2, k2, 2/2 LPC, p2, 2/2 RPC, k2, p2.

RNDS 24 – 26: (P2, k2) 4 times, p2.

RND 27: Rep rnd 21.

RND 28: Rep rnd 6.

RND 29: P2, k2, 2/2 LPC, p2, 2/2 RPC, k2, p2.

RND 30: Rep rnd 1.

RND 31: Rep rnd 3.

RNDS 32 – 36: Rep rnd 1.

RND 37: Rep rnd 3.

Kindling Stockings (Left Foot) Chart Instructions

RNDS 1 – 2: (P2, k2) 4 times, p2. (18 sts)

RND 3: P2, k2, p2, 2/2/2 RPC, p2, k2, p2.

RND 4: Rep rnd 1.

RND 5: P2, k2, 2/2 RC, p2, 2/2 LC, k2, p2.

RND 6: (P2, k6) 2 times, p2.

RND 7: P2, 2/2 RPC, k2, p2, k2, 2/2 LPC, p2.

RNDS 8 – 9: Rep rnd 1.

RNDS 10 – 15: Rep rnds 4–9.

RND 16: Rep rnd 1.

RND 17: P2, k2, p2, 6 WC, p2, k2, p2.

RNDS 18 – 20: Rep rnd 1.

RND 21: P2, 2/2 LC, k2, p2, k2, 2/2 RC, p2.

RND 22: Rep rnd 6.

RND 23: P2, k2, 2/2 LPC, p2, 2/2 RPC, k2, p2.

RNDS 24 – 29: Rep rnds 18–23.

RND 30: Rep rnd 1.

RND 31: Rep rnd 3.

RNDS 32 – 36: Rep rnd 1.

RND 37: Rep rnd 3.

Kindling Stockings Schematic

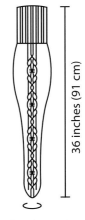

36 inches (91 cm)

7 inches (18 cm)

Kindling Stockings Chart Key

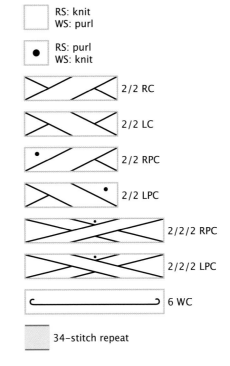

RS: knit
WS: purl

RS: purl
WS: knit

2/2 RC

2/2 LC

2/2 RPC

2/2 LPC

2/2/2 RPC

2/2/2 LPC

6 WC

34-stitch repeat

Kindling Stockings Right Chart

Kindling Stockings Left Chart

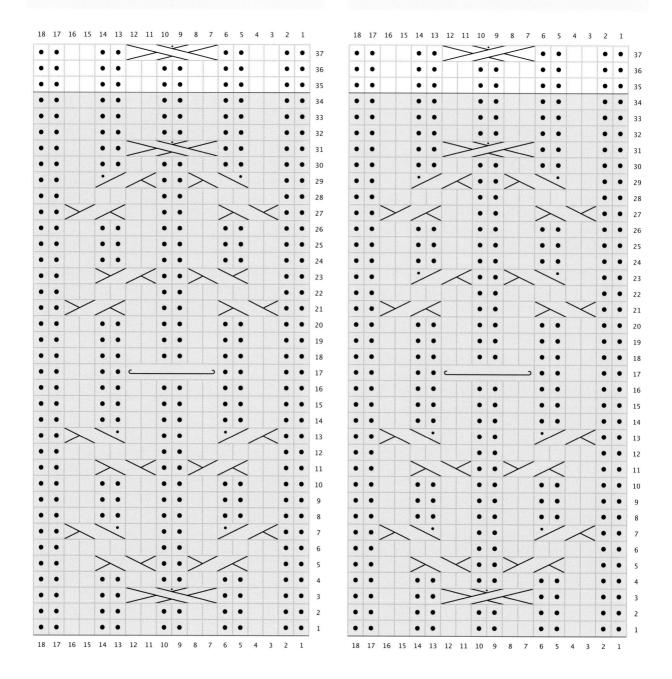

Cloud Cover Hood

Cloud Cover is a button-up neck warmer with a built-in hood. Designed to be worn like a mountain wears clouds, this neck warmer protects against the harsh winter cold and wind. Cloud Cover will help you beat the elements in cozy style. This pattern is charted and includes written instructions.

CONSTRUCTION

This hood is worked flat and seamed together with crochet slip stitches, though you could also seam it using a whip stitch, if you'd prefer. The neck ribbing and hood ribbing are picked up and worked in rib stitch. The button bands are made last.

A long circular needle is used so you can leave live stitches on reserve, on the circular, while working the right and left neck panels of the neck warmer.

SKILL LEVEL

- Complex

SIZE

- One size, for teen or adult

FINISHED MEASUREMENTS

Circumference
- 22 inches (56 cm), blocked

Height
- 16 inches (40.5 cm)

Button bands
- 7 inches (18 cm)

Hood depth
- 8½ inches (21.5 cm)

MATERIALS

Yarn
- Bulky weight, Red Heart Hygge (70% acrylic, 30% nylon), 212 yds (194 m) per 227-g skein

Yardage
- 275 yards (251.5 m)

Shown In
- Cloud colorway (2 skeins)

Any bulky weight yarn can be used for this pattern.

Needles

Hood body
- US 10½ (6.5 mm) 32-inch (80-cm) circular needle, or size needed to obtain gauge

Ribbing
- US 9 (5.5 mm) 32-inch (80-cm) circular needle, or two sizes down from needle you make gauge with

Notions
- 3 (1-inch [2.5-cm]) buttons
- Cable needle
- Sewing needle
- Stitch marker
- Tapestry needle
- Scissors
- Blocking materials

(continued)

GAUGE

15 sts x 16 rnds = 4 inches (10 cm) in cable pattern using larger needle (blocked)

SPECIAL TECHNIQUES

Crochet slip stitch (for seaming hood) (page 166)

Picking up and knitting stitches (page 170)

CABLE ABBREVIATIONS

All other abbreviations can be found on page 164.

- 2/1 LC = 2/1 left cable
- 2/1 LPC = 2/1 left purl cable
- 2/1 RC = 2/1 right cable
- 2/1 RPC = 2/1 right purl cable
- 2/2 LC = 2/2 left cable
- 2/2 LPC = 2/2 left purl cable
- 2/2 RC = 2/2 right cable
- 2/2 RPC = 2/2 right purl cable

SPECIAL STITCHES

- **2/1 LC:** Sl next 2 sts to CN and place at front of work, k1, then k2 from CN.
- **2/1 LPC:** Sl next 2 sts to CN and place at front of work, p1, then k2 from CN.
- **2/1 RC:** Sl next st to CN and place at back of work, k2, then k1 from CN.
- **2/1 RPC:** Sl next st to CN and place at back of work, k2, then p1 from CN.
- **2/2 LC:** Sl next 2 sts to CN and place at front of work, k2, then k2 from CN.
- **2/2 LPC:** Sl next 2 sts to CN and place at front of work, p2, then k2 from CN.
- **2/2 RC:** Sl next 2 sts to CN and place at back of work, k2, then k2 from CN.
- **2/2 RPC:** Sl next 2 sts to CN and place at back of work, k2, then p2 from CN.

Cloud Cover Hood Pattern

HOOD BODY

With larger needle, CO 114 sts.

Work rows 1–33 of Cloud Cover Hood Chart A (page 161) over first 18 sts, work Cloud Cover Hood Chart B (page 162) over the next 78 sts (the repeat section of Chart B repeats 4 times), work Chart A again over the last 18 sts. [33 rows]

RIGHT NECK PANEL

Work rows 1–8 of Cloud Cover Hood Chart C (page 163) over the first 18 sts of Hood Body. Leave the rem 96 sts on hold on the center of your circular needle. [8 rows]

Bind off on the RS in pattern. Break yarn.

LEFT NECK PANEL

With the RS facing, sl the last 18 sts of the Hood Body onto the empty end of your circular needle. [18 sts] Leave the rem 78 sts on hold.

Work rows 1–8 of Chart C. [8 rows]

Bind off on the RS in pattern. Break yarn.

HOOD RIBBING

With RS facing, the cast-on edge at the bottom, and using the smaller needle, pu & k7 sts from the left edge of the right neck panel (E), work across the 78 sts that were previously on hold as follows: K2, (p2, k2) 19 times, pu & k7 sts from the right edge of the left neck panel (F). [92 sts]

ROW 1 (WS): K3, (p2, k2) 22 times, k1.

ROW 2 (RS): P3, (k2, p2) 22 times, p1.

ROWS 3 – 10: Rep rows 1–2, four times.

ROW 11: Rep row 1.

Bind off loosely on the RS in pattern. Break yarn.

Fold the ribbing down, with the RS of ribbing facing and pin it down at both ends.

(continued)

Cloud Cover Hood Construction Diagram

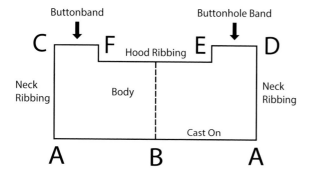

SEAM HOOD

Fold the Hood Body together RS facing at (B), so that both (A) points line up evenly. Use a crochet hook to sl st the two halves together at the cast-on edge. [57 sts]

Break yarn. Turn hood RS out.

NECK RIBBING

With RS facing turn hood so that the top of the hood is pointed down. Using the smaller needle, pu & k80 sts evenly across the neck edge of the hood (beginning at C and ending at D) as follows: pick up 1 st from the first row, skip a row, pick up 1 st from every row until 2 rows from the end, skip a row, pick up 1 st in the last row.

ROW 1 (WS): P3, (k2, p2) 19 times, p1.

ROW 2 (RS): K3, (p2, k2) 19 times, k1.

ROWS 3 – 4: Rep rows 1–2.

ROW 5: Rep row 1.

Bind off loosely on the RS in pattern. Break yarn.

BUTTONHOLE BAND

With RS facing and starting at the bottom of the neck ribbing on the right side of the hood, pu & k6 sts from the neck ribbing (1 st in each row), pu & k18 sts from the right neck panel (1 st in each st), pu & k6 sts from the folded hood ribbing, going through both layers of the hood ribbing at once. This will secure the collar permanently. [30 sts]

ROW 1 (WS): P2, (k2, p2) 7 times.

ROW 2 (RS): K2, *p1, yo, k2tog, k1, (p2, k2) twice; rep from * once more, p1, yo, k2tog, k1.

ROW 3: Rep row 1.

ROW 4: K2, (p2, k2) 7 times.

ROW 5: Rep row 1.

Bind off loosely on the RS in pattern. Break yarn.

BUTTON BAND

With RS facing and starting at the left side of the hood, pu & k6 sts from the folded hood ribbing, going through both layers of the hood ribbing at once. This will secure the collar permanently. Pu & k18 sts from the left neck panel (1 st in each st), pu & k6 sts from the neck ribbing (1 st in each row). [30 sts]

ROW 1 (WS): P2, (k2, p2) 7 times.

ROW 2 (RS): K2, (p2, k2) 7 times.

ROWS 3 – 4: Rep rows 1–2.

ROW 5: Rep row 1.

Bind off loosely on the RS in pattern. Break yarn.

FINISHING

Weave in all ends. Block to finished measurements. Once completely dry, unpin and sew on buttons to correspond with the buttonholes.

Cloud Cover Hood Chart A Instructions

ROW 1 (WS): (K2, p2) 4 times, k2. [18 sts]

ROW 2 (RS): (P2, k2) 4 times, p2.

ROW 3: Rep row 1.

ROW 4: P2, k2, p2, 2/1 LPC, 2/1 RPC, p2, k2, p2.

ROW 5: K2, p2, k3, p4, k3, p2, k2.

ROW 6: P2, 2/1 LPC, p2, 2/2 RC, p2, 2/1 RPC, p2.

ROW 7: K3, p2, k2, p4, k2, p2, k3.

ROW 8: P3, (2/1 LPC, 2/1 RPC) 2 times, p3.

ROW 9: K4, p4, k2, p4, k4.

ROW 10: P4, 2/2 LC, p2, 2/2 LC, p4.

ROW 11: Rep row 9.

ROW 12: P2, 2/2 RPC, 2/1 LPC, 2/1 RPC, 2/2 LPC, p2.

ROW 13: Rep row 5.

ROW 14: P2, k2, p3, 2/2 RC, p3, k2, p2.

ROW 15: Rep row 5.

ROW 16: P2, 2/2 LPC, 2/1 RPC, 2/1 LPC, 2/2 RPC, p2.

ROW 17: Rep row 9.

ROW 18: Rep row 10.

ROW 19: Rep row 9.

ROW 20: P2, 2/2 RPC, 2/1 LC, 2/1 RC, 2/2 LPC, p2.

ROW 21: Rep row 5.

ROWS 22 – 29: Rep rows 14–21.

ROW 30: Rep row 14.

ROW 31: Rep row 5.

ROW 32: Rep row 16.

ROW 33: Rep row 9.

Cloud Cover Hood Chart B (Repeat) Instructions

ROW 1 (WS): (P2, k2) 3 times, p2, *(k2, p2) 4 times; rep from * 4 times. [78 sts]

ROW 2 (RS): *(K2, p2) 4 times; rep from * 4 times, (k2, p2) 3 times, k2.

ROW 3: Rep row 1.

ROW 4: *K2, p2, 2/1 LPC, 2/1 RPC, p2, k2, p2; rep from * 4 times, k2, p2, 2/1 LPC, 2/1 RPC, p2, k2.

ROW 5: P2, k3, p4, k3, p2, *k2, p2, k3, p4, k3, p2; rep from * 4 times.

ROW 6: *2/1 LPC, p2, 2/2 RC, p2, 2/1 RPC, p2; rep from * 4 times, 2/1 LPC, p2, 2/2 RC, p2, 2/1 RPC.

ROW 7: K1, p2, k2, p4, k2, p2, k1, *k3, p2, k2, p4, k2, p2, k1; rep from * 4 times.

ROW 8: *P1, (2/1 LPC, 2/1 RPC) 2 times, p3; rep from * 4 times, p1, (2/1 LPC, 2/1 RPC) 2 times, p1.

ROW 9: (K2, p4) 2 times, k2, *k4, (p4, k2) 2 times; rep from * 4 times.

ROW 10: *(P2, 2/2 LC) 2 times, p4; rep from * 4 times, (p2, 2/2 LC) 2 times, p2.

ROW 11: Rep row 9.

ROW 12: *2/2 RPC, 2/1 LPC, 2/1 RPC, 2/2 LPC, p2; rep from * 4 times, 2/2 RPC, 2/1 LPC, 2/1 RPC, 2/2 LPC.

ROW 13: Rep row 5.

ROW 14: *K2, p3, 2/2 RC, p3, k2, p2; rep from * 4 times, k2, p3, 2/2 RC, p3, k2.

ROW 15: Rep row 5.

ROW 16: *2/2 LPC, 2/1 RPC, 2/1 LPC, 2/2 RPC, p2; rep from * 4 times, 2/2 LPC, 2/1 RPC, 2/1 LPC, 2/2 RPC.

ROW 17: Rep row 9.

ROW 18: Rep row 10.

ROW 19: Rep row 9.

(continued)

Cloud Cover Hood (Continued)

ROW 20: *2/2 RPC, 2/1 LC, 2/1 RC, 2/2 LPC, p2; rep from * 4 times, 2/2 RPC, 2/1 LC, 2/1 RC, 2/2 LPC.

ROW 21: Rep row 5.

ROW 22: Rep row 14.

ROW 23: Rep row 5.

ROW 24: Rep row 16.

ROW 25: Rep row 9.

ROW 26: Rep row 10.

ROW 27: Rep row 9.

ROW 28: *P1, (2/1 RPC, 2/1 LPC) 2 times, p3; rep from * 4 times, p1, (2/1 RPC, 2/1 LPC) 2 times, p1.

ROW 29: Rep row 7.

ROW 30: *2/1 RPC, p2, 2/2 RC, p2, 2/1 LPC, p2; rep from * 4 times, 2/1 RPC, p2, 2/2 RC, p2, 2/1 LPC.

ROW 31: Rep row 5.

ROW 32: *K2, p2, 2/1 RPC, 2/1 LPC, p2, k2, p2; rep from * 4 times, k2, p2, 2/1 RPC, 2/1 LPC, p2, k2.

ROW 33: Rep row 1.

Cloud Cover Hood Chart C Instructions

ROW 1 (RS): P4, 2/2 LC, p2, 2/2 LC, p4. [18 sts]

ROW 2 (WS): K4, p4, k2, p4, k4.

ROW 3: P3, (2/1 RPC, 2/1 LPC) 2 times, p3.

ROW 4: K3, p2, k2, p4, k2, p2, k3.

ROW 5: P2, 2/1 RPC, p2, 2/2 RC, p2, 2/1 LPC, p2.

ROW 6: K2, p2, k3, p4, k3, p2, k2.

ROW 7: P2, k2, p2, 2/1 RPC, 2/1 LPC, p2, k2, p2.

ROW 8: (K2, p2) 4 times, k2.

Cloud Cover Hood Schematic

8 ½ inches (21.5 cm)

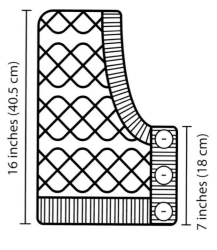

16 inches (40.5 cm)

7 inches (18 cm)

22 inches (56 cm)

Cloud Cover Hood Chart Key

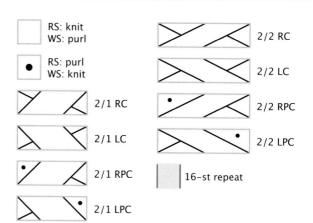

	RS: knit WS: purl
	RS: purl WS: knit
	2/1 RC
	2/1 LC
	2/1 RPC
	2/1 LPC
	2/2 RC
	2/2 LC
	2/2 RPC
	2/2 LPC
	16-st repeat

Cloud Cover Hood Chart A

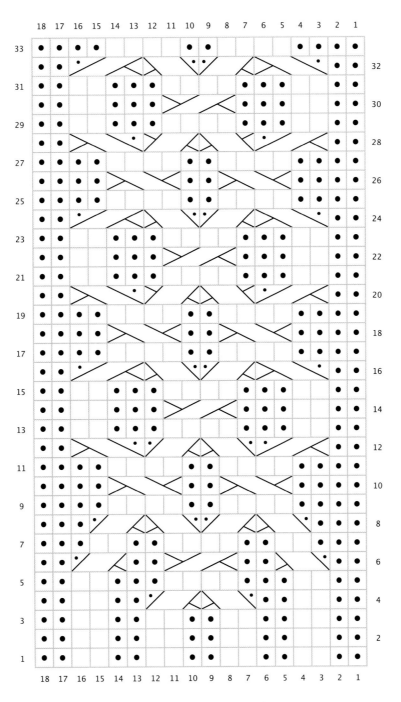

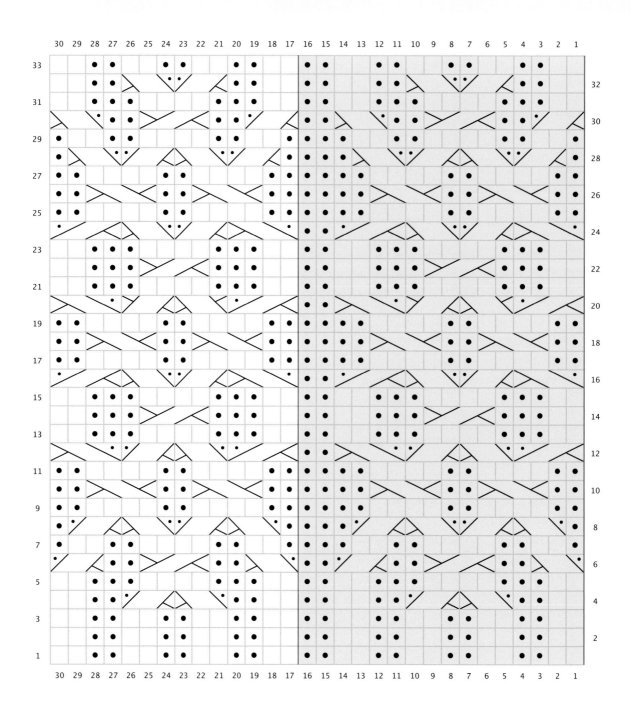

Cloud Cover Hood Chart C

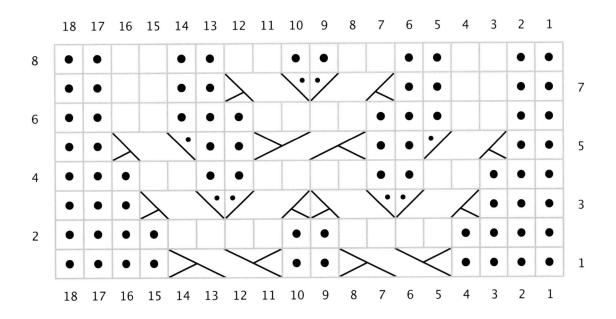

ABBREVIATIONS

BN = back needle

BO = bind off

BOR = beginning of round

CDD = center double decrease

ch = chain stitch using a crochet hook

CN = cable needle

CO = cast on

DPN = double pointed needle

FN = front needle

k = knit

k2tog = knit two stitches together

kfb = knit into the front and back of the same stitch

LH = left hand

LLI = left lifted increase

m = marker

m1L = make one left

m1R = make one right

mb = make bobble

p = purl

p2tog = purl two stitches together

pm = place marker

pu = pick up

rem = remaining

rep = repeat

RH = right hand

RLI = right lifted increase

rnd = round

RS = right side

sk2p = slip one stitch, knit next two stitches together, pass the slipped stitch over

sl = slip

sl1p = slip one stitch purlwise

sm = slip marker

ssk = slip one stitch, slip the next stitch, knit together

st(s) = stitch(es)

swk = shadow wrap knit

swp = shadow wrap purl

tbl = through the back loop

WS = wrong side

wyib = with yarn in back

wyif = with yarn in front

yo = yarn over

TECHNIQUES

3-NEEDLE BIND-OFF

STEP 1: Ensure that you have an equal number of stitches on both of your working needles.

Place the needles with the stitches parallel to one another, with right sides toward each other, wrong sides facing out.

STEP 2: Insert your empty needle (the third needle) knitwise through the first stitch on the front needle, and the first stitch on the back needle, as if to knit.

STEP 3: Knit these two stitches together, so there is now one stitch on the third needle and one fewer stitch than you started with on each of the other two needles.

STEP 4: Do the same thing again, knitting what's now the first stitch on both needles into one stitch.

STEP 5: Lift the first stitch on the third needle over the second stitch and over the top of the needle, just as you do in a normal bind-off method.

STEP 6: Continue in this manner until you're down to one loop on the third needle and no loops on the other needles. Cut your yarn, slide the last loop off the needle and put the yarn through the loop. Pull tightly.

BOBBLES

Insert the needle into the stitch you'll be working your bobble into, k1, (yo, k1) 3 times into the stitch, keeping your stitches nice and loose. There will be 7 sts on your needle. Drop the final stitch off the LH needle. Turn work to WS and purl these 7 loops together. Turn work to RS. Slip the resulting stitch back onto the RH needle purlwise. Secure this bobble by inserting the LH needle tip into the left leg of the stitch one row below the bobble, from left to right. Knit into this stitch, pass the loop above the bobble over this knit stitch. The bobble is now secure and should appear on the RS of your work.

CABLE CAST-ON

STEP 1: Insert the RH needle between the first and second stitch on the LH needle.

STEP 2: Knit a stitch onto the right needle, just as you normally would, except do not remove the stitch from the left needle.

STEP 3: Now there's a stitch on the right needle. Without twisting it, place that stitch onto the left needle.

STEP 4: Repeat steps 1 through 3 until you have cast on the number of stitches you need.

CROCHET CHAIN

STEP 1: Make a slip knot on your crochet hook, or place an existing stitch onto your hook. With the slip knot (or existing loop) on the crochet hook, grasp the knot/loop between the thumb and middle fingers of your left hand. The slip knot/loop should face you. The working yarn, the strand coming from the ball, should flow over your index finger, between your index and middle finger and across your palm, then to the back again between your ring and little finger. This feels awkward at first but will help you tension the yarn as you make stitches and need more yarn from the ball. Grasp your crochet hook in your right hand using a pencil grip, knife grip or whatever feels most comfortable to you. To start, keep the crochet hook facing upward. You will be rotating it as you make chain stitches, so grip the hook tightly enough to maintain control but loosely enough to move easily.

STEP 2: Loop the working yarn over the hook from back to front. Either use your left hand to wrap the yarn over the crochet hook from behind and then over the top or use your right hand to manipulate your hook to do the same thing. This maneuver is called "yarn round hook" or "yarn over."

STEP 3: Rotate your crochet hook by about one quarter turn counterclockwise as you loop the yarn to prepare for hooking it. It's okay to turn it more if you need to, but the goal is to make each move as precise and fluid as possible. Pull the hook down and through the current loop on the hook. As you just finish drawing the yarn through, you will likely find it easier to complete the stitch if you return the hook to its original position facing upward.

STEP 4: You have now "chained one," making one chain stitch. To make another chain stitch, yarn over the hook, and draw up a loop. Repeat this as many times as necessary. As you crochet, move your thumb and index fingers up the newly formed chain stitches, staying just a stitch or two away from the loop on the hook. This will help you have more control and better tension as you make your stitches: not too tight, not too loose. As you work, you'll find a rhythm in rotating the crochet hook as you yarn over, and then rotating it back as you draw through a loop. Having a rhythm makes the process easier and faster.

CROCHET SLIP STITCH

STEP 1: To start your slip stitch, you can work a slip stitch at just about any point after you begin your project. If you already have an active loop on your crochet hook, insert your hook into the spot where you want to crochet the slip stitch. Then hook your yarn.

STEP 2: Pull the yarn up through your project.

STEP 3: Finally, draw the newly created loop through the active loop on your hook. After you try these steps a few times, it will become almost like a single motion. The slip stitch is now complete.

GERMAN TWISTED LONGTAIL CAST-ON

STEP 1: To get started, you need only one of your knitting needles. This method uses a long tail, so you need to estimate how much yarn you need for the tail. Begin with a slip knot on the needle. Hold the yarn like a slingshot with the long tail looped over your thumb. Drape the two strands of yarn over your thumb and index finger and then hold it taut with the rest of your fingers. Hold the slip knot in place with your index finger as you hold the knitting needle. This is the same way you hold the two strands of yarn for a longtail cast-on (page 168).

STEP 2: Dip the needle around and under both strands of yarn that are wrapped around your thumb.

STEP 3: To complete the twist, insert the needle down into the loop near your thumb. Catch the side of the yarn loop that's away from you and then bring it up toward you.

STEP 4: Next, bring the needle to the outside of the yarn looped around your finger. Dip the needle under the yarn to catch it.

STEP 5: Bring the needle with the yarn toward you and draw it through the small gap in the twisted loop from your thumb. Depending on how you are holding your yarn and the tension on the twist, it can be tricky to spot this little window at first. It will be close to the slip stitch (or previous stitch as you add more stitches). As you become familiar with the process, it gets easier to see where to draw the needle through.

STEP 6: When the yarn is through the twisted gap, let the loop of yarn drop from your thumb. Use your thumb and finger to pull the strands of yarn, tightening the newly cast-on stitch. The stitch should be able to slide freely on the needle, without looking or feeling too loose. Position the strands of yarn over your thumb and finger again, just as they were when you started. As you get into the rhythm of casting on, your thumb will naturally start to go from dropping the loop to tightening the new stitch to finally returning to the starting position.

STEP 7: Repeat the steps above to add more stitches to your needle.

I-CORD

You should have 3 stitches on the right-hand DPN and the yarn should be attached to the left stitch. Slide the stitches from one end of the needle to the other. Without turning the needle, place the needle in your left hand. The yarn should be coming from the far-left stitch. Pulling the yarn so that it is snug, knit the 3 stitches from the left to the right needle. Everything is normal except that the yarn is coming from the last stitch in the row instead of the first when you begin knitting this row. When you have knit all 3 stitches onto the right needle, slide the stitches from one end of the DPN to the other. Repeat these steps, pulling the yarn snug at the beginning of each row to insure even stitches. To bind off, k1, k2tog, pass the second stitch over the first stitch. Break yarn and pull through the remaining stitch.

JENY'S SURPRISINGLY STRETCHY BIND-OFF

Knit or purl the first stitch as called for in your pattern. Then work as follows:

Before a Knit Stitch

STEP 1: Yo backward (bring yarn from back to front over right needle), then k1.

STEP 2: On your right needle, pull stitches 2 and 3 over stitch 1; one stitch bound off, one stitch on the right needle.

Repeats steps 1 and 2 as established until all stitches are bound off.

Before a Purl Stitch

STEP 1: Yo (bring yarn from front to back over right needle, then to front again), then p1.

STEP 2: On your right needle, pull stitches 2 and 3 over stitch 1; one stitch bound off, one stitch on the right needle.

Repeat steps 1 and 2 as established until all stitches are bound off.

JUDY'S MAGIC CAST-ON

STEP 1: Leaving a long tail, make your slip knot and place it on your circular needle. Hold the tail and working yarn as you would for a longtail cast-on (page 168), but with the positions reversed. Hold both needle tips together and you are ready to begin! (Hold needles together for the duration of the cast-on.)

STEP 2: Bring needle 1 over the tail, then up underneath it, catching it over needle 1.

STEP 3: This will create a loop around needle 1. Pull the loop so that it is snug. You have cast on a stitch.

STEP 4: Now bring needle 2 over the working yarn, then up underneath it, catching the yarn over needle 2.

STEP 5: This will create a loop around needle 2. Pull the loop so that it is snug. Another stitch created.

STEP 6: Repeat steps 2–5 until you have cast on the desired number of stitches (e.g., 20 stitches, 10 on needle 1 and 10 on needle 2).

STEP 7: Now you can begin knitting the stitches on needle 1. Make sure the tail is tucked behind the working yarn when you knit the first stitch. (Note that the needles are now rearranged for a Magic Loop and the stitches which were on needle 2 are now on the cable.)

STEP 8: Now knit the stitches on needle 2 through the back loop as they will be twisted from the cast-on.

STEP 9: You will now be ready to work toe increases as instructed in your sock or stocking pattern.

KITCHENER STITCH

SET-UP: Place stitches on 2 parallel needles with wrong sides facing each other, right side facing out. Thread a length of working yarn three times the length of the pieces you are joining onto a tapestry needle. Hold work so you have a front knitting needle and back knitting needle. Insert the tapestry needle through the first stitch on front needle as if to purl, pull yarn through, leaving stitch on needle. Next, insert the tapestry needle through first stitch on the back needle as if to knit, then pull yarn through, leaving the stitch on the needle.

STEP 1: Keeping the yarn under the needles at all times, insert the tapestry needle through the first stitch on the front needle as if to knit and take it off the needle. Then insert the tapestry needle through the second stitch on the front needle as if to purl and leave it on the needle; pull the yarn through.

STEP 2: Keeping the yarn under the needles, insert the tapestry needle through the first stitch on the back needle as if to purl and take it off the needle. Then insert the tapestry needle through the second stitch on the back needle as if to knit and leave it on the needle; pull yarn through.

STEP 3: Chant this to yourself as you work: Knit off, purl on (front needle). Purl off, knit on (back needle). Remember to keep the yarn below the needles and match the tension to your knitting tension. If you prefer, you may work 4 or 5 stitches off both needles (always ending with Step 2), then go back and adjust the tension before continuing, or adjust the tension at the end if you have two short edges.

LONGTAIL CAST-ON

STEP 1: Before you make your slip knot you will need to leave a "long tail" that will accommodate the number of stitches you are creating. The tail should be roughly three times the width of your finished piece of knitting.

STEP 2: Make a slip knot, leaving the appropriate length of yarn for the tail. Place the slip knot on one of your needles and snug it up by tugging lightly on the yarn tails. Hold the needle in your right hand with the needle tip pointing to the left. This slipknot counts as your first stitch.

STEP 3: Grasp the two yarn ends below the slip knot in your left hand. Push your left thumb and forefinger through the two strands (the long tail should be over your thumb, the working yarn over your forefinger).

STEP 4: Spread the fingers apart and lower the needle so that the yarn makes a V between the thumb and forefinger. You can use the forefinger of your right hand to hold the slip knot on the needle.

STEP 5: Pass the needle under the yarn around the thumb, over the top of the yarn around the forefinger, and back through the yarn around the thumb.

STEP 6: Draw the thumb out from the yarn loop and tug lightly on the yarn tails to tighten up your stitch.

Repeat steps 5 and 6 until you have cast on the required number of stitches. Remember that the slip-knot counts as your first stitch.

LONGTAIL TUBULAR CAST-ON

SET UP: Begin by setting up your yarn as for the Longtail Cast-On technique (page 168): Make a slip knot with a tail approximately three times the length of your cast-on row, slip it onto your needle and hold the yarn with the tail wrapping down around your thumb, and the working yarn (attached to the ball) wrapping up around your index finger, with both yarns held in place with your other fingers. The slip knot is the first cast-on stitch. We will call the working yarn the "top yarn" and the tail yarn the "bottom yarn" because this is how they're placed as you work the cast-on. As a rule, stitches in this cast-on must always switch between knit and purl. In this case, we're treating the first stitch (the slip knot) as a knit stitch, so our first step will be a purl cast-on stitch.

CAST ON A PURL STITCH: To cast on a purl stitch, bring the needle up over the top yarn, around behind the top yarn and down over the bottom yarn, around behind the bottom yarn and up back behind the top yarn and over to the front. Then, pull the two yarns to tighten up the stitch on the needle. The stitch will have a little bump below it like a purl stitch.

CAST ON A KNIT STITCH: For a knit stitch, it's basically the reverse of a purl stitch. Bring the needle down over the bottom yarn, around behind the bottom yarn and up, up over the top yarn, around behind the top yarn and down, back behind the bottom yarn, and under to the front. Tighten the stitch by pulling both yarns snug; the knit stitch will have no bump below it.

ENDING CAST-ON: You can end after a knit or a purl, depending on your pattern. Cast on the number of stitches needed.

SET-UP ROW 1: This cast-on method requires two set-up rows, which are always worked flat, even if your pattern is in the round! Turn your needle to work the first set-up row flat.

You'll be working the stitches during the set-up rows with your working yarn. While knitting or purling, hold the tail yarn snugly while working the first few stitches, to hold things in place. This cast-on is very loosely held together and can fall apart if you let the tail go while beginning the set-up row.

For our example, the first stitch will be a knit stitch; if your first stitch is a purl stitch, skip to the purl stitch instruction below.

To work each knit stitch, knit through the back loop, because the knit stitches are twisted on the needle (the front loop goes to the left instead of to the right) so knitting through the back will orient them correctly. For the first knit stitch, be sure to hold the tail snugly while working it, then pull it to tighten the stitch on the needle afterward.

To work each purl stitch, bring the working yarn to the front, then slip the stitch purlwise. Bring yarn to the back to work the next knit stitch, knitting through the back loop. Work the whole row in that pattern: (K1 through the back loop, sl1wyif) to end, always knitting the knit stitches and slipping the purl stitches.

SET-UP ROW 2: Turn to work the second row flat. The second row is worked the same as the first, except that the knit stitches are oriented correctly now so they don't need to be knit through the back loops. So, beginning with whichever stitch is first for you: (Knit the knit stitches, slip the purl stitches with yarn in front) to end. We started with a knit stitch, so next is slipping the purl stitch with yarn in front. Repeat to the end, working the knit stitches normally. The cast-on is now finished. Either turn to work your first normal row flat or join to work in the round.

Note: If joining in the round, you will need to seam these rows when you're finished. Work normal K1, P1 ribbing, knitting the knit stitches and purling the purl stitches.

PICKING UP AND KNITTING STITCHES
ALONG A HORIZONTAL EDGE: Insert your needle, from front to back, into the center of the stitch closest to the cast-on (or bind-off) edge; wrap the working yarn around the needle counter-clockwise as if to knit; use the tip of the needle to pull that yarn through to the front of the fabric. 1 stitch is now picked up. Repeat as directed in the pattern.

ALONG A VERTICAL EDGE (STOCKI-NETTE): Insert your needle, from front to back, between the last and second-to-last columns of stitches; wrap the working yarn around the needle counter-clockwise as if to knit; use the tip of the needle to pull that yarn through to the front of the fabric.

Note: When picking up stitches along a vertical edge, the new stitches will run perpendicular to the existing stitches. Because the stitch and row gauges are typically unequal, you will not pick up a stitch for each row along the vertical edge of the fabric. Refer to the pattern for how many stitches to pick up over how many rows.

ALONG A VERTICAL EDGE (GARTER STITCH): Insert your needle, from front to back, between the ridges of garter, between the last and second-to-last columns of stitches; wrap the working yarn around the needle counter-clockwise as if to knit; use the tip of the needle to pull that yarn through to the front of the fabric.

Note: When picking up stitches along a vertical edge, the new stitches will run perpendicular to the existing stitches. Because the stitch and row gauges are typically unequal, you will not pick up a stitch for each row along the vertical edge of the fabric. Refer to the pattern for how many stitches to pick up over how many rows.

PICOT
CO 2 sts using a cable cast-on (page 165), BO 2 sts.

PROVISIONAL CAST-ON
In this method, you will pick up and knit stitches into the back of a crochet chain with the working yarn, resulting in a completed row of stitches. To open up your chain and make it easier to see and work with, try using a crochet hook that's a size or two larger than your project's recommended needle size. With waste yarn (or knotting cord) and your crochet hook, chain the desired number of stitches. (I recommend that you chain a few extra so if you miss one, you won't have to start all over again.) Clip a locking stitch marker into the final chain and cut the waste yarn.

Take a good look at your chain. It has a flat side with a series of Vs that look like a typical knitted bound-off edge. Flip the chain over and notice the line of bumps along the back of the chain—they look a little like the ridges along the spine of a dinosaur. They are the loops you'll knit into. With your working yarn—leaving the desired length of tail and beginning in the first stitch you chained (not the end with your locking marker)—knit into the back bumps of your chain for the desired number of cast-on stitches.

Note: When the first row you knitted into your chain is released from the chain, it will not appear as a knit or purl. When the time comes to remove this provisional cast-on, take out the locking stitch marker and unzip (or unravel) the chain. Place the live loops of exposed stitches onto your needle and proceed as your pattern instructs you.

SEWN TUBULAR BIND-OFF
SET UP: Measure out a tail at least three times the length to be bound off, break yarn and thread the tail onto a tapestry needle.

STEP 1: Working from right to left, insert the tapestry needle purlwise into the first stitch (a knit stitch) and pull the yarn through.

STEP 2: Holding the tapestry needle behind the first stitch, insert it knitwise into the next stitch (a purl stitch) and pull the yarn through.

STEP 3: Return the tapestry needle to the front and insert it knitwise into the first (knit) stitch, slipping this stitch off the knitting needle.

STEP 4: With the tapestry needle at the front of the work, skip the first stitch on the knitting needle (a purl stitch) and insert the tapestry needle purlwise into the next stitch (a knit stitch). Pull the yarn through.

STEP 5: Insert the tapestry needle purlwise into the first stitch (a purl stitch) and pull the yarn through, slipping this stitch off the knitting needle.

STEP 6: Holding the tapestry needle behind the first stitch on the knitting needle (a knit stitch), insert the tapestry needle knitwise into the next stitch (a purl stitch) and pull the yarn through.

Repeat steps 3–6 until 2 stitches remain. Work step 3 once more, so 1 stitch remains. Insert the tapestry needle purlwise into the last stitch and pull the yarn through, drawing tight to secure.

SHADOW WRAP KNIT (SWK)

If working a SWK on a single stitch, you will create a Twin Stitch. If working a SWK on a Twin Stitch, you will need to create a Triplet Stitch.

SHADOW WRAP PURL (SWP)

If working a SWP on a single stitch, you will create a Twin Stitch. If working a SWP on a Twin Stitch, you will need to create a Triplet Stitch.

TWIN STITCH (ON THE KNIT SIDE)

Hold your yarn to the back. Insert RH needle tip purlwise into right leg of the stitch one row below the stitch you're wrapping. Lift this loop up and place onto LH needle purlwise. Knit this loop and place that knit stitch back onto LH needle purlwise. You now have 2 loops coming from the stitch 1 row below. This is called a Twin Stitch. After completing the wrap, turn your work.

Note: The wrap should always be on the LH needle before turning.

TWIN STITCH (ON THE PURL SIDE)

Hold your yarn to the front. Slip stitch from LH needle onto RH needle purlwise. Insert LH needle tip into purl bump directly below the stitch on RH needle. Stretch out this loop to loosen it, leaving it on LH needle. Purl this loop and remove from needle. You now have 2 loops coming from the stitch 1 row below.

This is called a Twin Stitch. After completing the wrap, place both loops back onto the LH needle and turn your work.

Note: The wrap should always be on the LH needle before turning.

TRIPLET STITCH (ON THE KNIT SIDE)

Hold your yarn to the back. Insert RH needle tip purlwise into the right leg of the Twin Stitch one row below the stitch you're wrapping. Lift this loop up and place onto LH needle purlwise. Knit this loop and place that knit stitch back onto LH needle purlwise. You now have 3 loops coming from the stitch 1 row below.

This is called a Triplet Stitch. The wrap should be on LH needle. Turn your work.

Note: The wrap should always be on the LH needle before turning.

TRIPLET STITCH (ON THE PURL SIDE)

Hold your yarn to the front. Slip Twin Stitch from LH needle onto RH needle purlwise. Insert LH needle tip into purl bump directly below the stitch on RH needle. Stretch out this loop to loosen it, leaving it on LH needle. Purl this loop and remove from needle. You now have 3 loops coming from the stitch 1 row below.

This is called a Triplet Stitch. Place this stitch back onto LH needle purlwise and turn your work.

Note: The wrap should always be on the LH needle before turning.

RESOURCES

Thank you to these yarn companies:

- KNITPICKS
  https://knitpicks.com/
- UNIVERSAL YARN
  https://universalyarn.com/
- JOANN
  https://joann.com/
- MALABRIGO
  https://malabrigoyarn.com/
- LION BRAND YARN
  https://lionbrand.com/
- WOOLFOLK
  https://woolfolkyarn.com/

Thank you to these wonderful knitters for their explanations of various techniques used in this book:

- SHIBUI KNITS
  https://shibuiknits.com/
- CRAFT YARN COUNCIL
  https://craftyarncouncil.com/
- THE SPRUCE CRAFTS
  https://thesprucecrafts.com/
- POM POM
  https://pompommag.com/
- PURL SOHO
  https://purlsoho.com/
- *CAST ON, BIND OFF* BY LESLIE ANN BESTOR
  https://goodreads.com/en/book/show/13422143-cast-on-bind-off

My talented father supplied the stunning handmade wood toggles and buttons for the Ice Chalet Cowl (page 74) and Cloud Cover Hood (page 155):

- GLENN DUNCAN OF GLENNWOOD CARVINGS
  http://glennwoodcarvings.net/

My local yarn shop was an incredible resource and supplied most of the yarn used in the sample patterns for this book. You gals are amazing!

- PURL2 WALLA WALLA
  https://purl2w2.com/

All of the indoor photography in this book was shot on location in a gorgeous Airbnb cabin owned by Tina Oliva.

ACKNOWLEDGMENTS

A heartfelt thank you to my patient husband, Jason, who was my support and sounding board as I worked on this book. To my kids, Zander, Zachary and Zoe, who had to share me with this books creation. To my daughter Zoe Hudson, who created all the schematics for this book and modeled all the knitwear for the photography. And speaking of photography, I have to thank my son Zachary Hudson, who assisted me on all the photo shoots. A huge thank-you to my book editor Emily Taylor, my pattern tech editor Cathy Susko and my sweater grader Becky Monahan, who were all critical to this process. I also want to thank Sarah Wutzke and Leah Sandven of Purl2 Walla Walla, my local yarn shop, for helping supply me with the yarn I used on many of the pattern samples in this book. A heartfelt thank-you to Amy Leistiko, who welcomed me into her home all those years ago, to show me the basics of knitting. And finally, a very special thank-you to Page Street for inviting me to write and publish my very first book.

ABOUT THE AUTHOR

KALURAH HUDSON is a self-taught knitwear designer and photographer living in the Pacific Northwest. A wife and mom of three, she loves to cook, bake, hike and photograph her many knit creations.

After working as a secretary in a large medical clinic and a small locally owned sewing shop, Kalurah looked for ways to help support her growing family and stay at home with her babies. So, While They Play Designs was born.

In 2008, she designed and self-published her first crochet pattern, Romantic Fingerless Gloves, on Etsy and Ravelry. The following year, she published her first knitting pattern, the Jazz Baby Headband. In 2010, she was thrilled to have her hooded neck warmer pattern published in *Vogue Knitting* in their Winter issue.

That same year also brought an exciting opportunity for Kalurah to join the up-and-coming yarn company KnitPicks and she began designing for their blooming Independent Pattern Designers program. She has had numerous designs published in their many books and collections, available on their website: knitpicks.com.

You can find Kalurah's self-published designs at: https://www.knitpicks.com/patterns/kalurah-hudson/c/30026801

She has also contributed knitting patterns to *Highland Knits: Knitwear Inspired by the Outlander Series*, published by Interweave in 2016.

Kalurah has collaborated with KnitCrate, Malabrigo and We Are Knitters®, as well as some very dear yarn dyers such as Julie of Julie Asselin Yarn, Frances of LeFrances Handmade & Fibre Art, Heather of Sew Happy Jane, Sara and Leah of Purls Before Wine and Wendy of Amanda Hope Yarn.

You can find Kalurah's designs on Ravelry.com, Etsy.com/shop/whiletheyplay and on her personal website: whiletheyplaydesigns.com.

Kalurah also has a YouTube channel where you can find many helpful tutorials and stitch videos: youtube.com/Whiletheyplay

FOLLOW KALURAH ON INSTAGRAM
@kalurah

FOLLOW KALURAH ON TWITTER
@kalurah

FOLLOW KALURAH ON PINTEREST
https://www.pinterest.com/whiletheyplay/

INDEX

A

abbreviations, 164
Aran weight yarn
    Aspens Asymmetric Shawl, 108–121
    Smokestack Ankle Socks, 59–64
Aspens Asymmetric Shawl
    chart A, 115
    chart A instructions, 110–111
    chart B, 116
    chart B instructions, 111–112
    chart C (left), 118
    chart C (right), 117
    chart C instructions, 112–113
    chart D (left), 120
    chart D (right), 119
    chart D instructions, 113–114
    chart E (left), 121
    chart E (right), 121
    chart E instructions, 114
    chart key, 115
    overview, 108
    pattern, 110
    schematic, 115

B

basic skill level: Snowbird Blanket Shawl, 27–31
Bräcken Frost Hat
    chart, 20
    chart instructions, 19
    chart key, 20
    overview, 17–18
    pattern, 18–19
    schematic, 19
bulky weight yarn
    Cloud Cover Hood, 155–163
    Ice Chalet Cowl, 74–79
    Snow Fern Cardigan, 32–55
    Storm Flurry Wrap, 139–147

C

Campfire Stories Fingerless Mitts
    chart instructions, 95–98
    chart key, 99
    chart (left BN bottom), 104
    chart (left BN top), 106
    chart (left FN bottom), 105
    chart (left FN top), 107

    chart (right BN bottom), 100
    chart (right BN top), 102
    chart (right FN bottom), 101
    chart (right FN top), 103
    overview, 93–94
    pattern, 94–95
    schematic, 99
Campfire Stories Hat
    chart instructions, 85–86
    chart key, 87
    chart (bottom left), 88
    chart (bottom right), 89
    chart (top left), 90
    chart (top right), 91
    overview, 83–84
    pattern, 84
    schematic, 87
charts
    Aspens Asymmetric Shawl, 115–121
    Bräcken Frost Hat, 20
    Campfire Stories Fingerless Mitts, 100–107
    Campfire Stories Hat, 88–91
    Cloud Cover Hood, 161–163
    Cross Country Hooded Infinity Cowl, 25
    Ice Chalet Cowl, 79
    Kindling Stockings, 154
    River Rock Throw, 127–129
    Smokestack Ankle Socks, 64
    Snowberry Hat, 69
    Snowbird Blanket Shawl, 30–31
    Snow Fern Cardigan, 38–55
    Snow Tracks Headband, 73
    Storm Flurry Wrap, 144–147
    Winter Dreamer Pullover, 137
Cloud Cover Hood
    chart A, 161
    chart A instructions, 159
    chart B, 162
    chart B (repeat) instructions, 159–160
    chart C, 163
    chart C instructions, 160
    chart key, 160
    construction diagram, 158
    overview, 155–156
    pattern, 156–158
    schematic, 160

complex skill level
    Aspens Asymmetric Shawl, 108–121
    Campfire Stories Fingerless Mitts, 93–107
    Campfire Stories Hat, 83–91
    Cloud Cover Hood, 155–163
    Ice Chalet Cowl, 74–79
    Kindling Stockings, 149–154
    Smokestack Ankle Socks, 59–64
    Snow Fern Cardigan, 32–55
    Winter Dreamer Pullover, 133–138
Craft Yarn Council, 13
Cross Country Hooded Infinity Cowl
    chart, 25
    chart instructions, 22–24
    chart key, 25
    overview, 21–22
    pattern, 22
    pattern grafting, 24
    schematic, 25

D

dropped stitches
    bobbles, 165
    fingers and, 13
    left-leaning cable, 11, 12
    right-leaning cable, 10–11
    sticky fibers and, 13
    tapered points and, 12

E

easy skill level: River Rock Throw, 123–129

F

fiber
    dropped stitches and, 13
    needle material and, 8
    selecting, 8

I

Ice Chalet Cowl
    chart, 79
    chart instructions, 77
    chart key, 78
    overview, 74–76
    pattern, 76–77
    schematic, 78
intermediate skill level
    Bräcken Frost Hat, 17–20

Cross Country Hooded Infinity
Cowl, 21–25
Snowberry Hat, 65–69
Snow Tracks Headband, 71–73
Storm Flurry Wrap, 139–147

K

Kindling Stockings
chart instructions (left foot), 153
chart instructions (right foot), 152
chart key, 153
chart (left), 154
chart (right), 154
overview, 149–150
pattern (make two), 150–152
schematic, 153

L

lace weight yarn: Kindling Stockings,
149–154

N

needles
cable needles, 9
double-pointed needles, 9
grooves, 9
interchangeable tips, 9
materials for, 8
rubberized, 9
selecting, 9
tapered points, 9, 12
U-shape in, 9

P

patterns
Aspens Asymmetric Shawl, 110
Bräcken Frost Hat, 18–19
Campfire Stories Fingerless Mitts,
94–95
Campfire Stories Hat, 84
Cloud Cover Hood, 156–158
Cross Country Hooded Infinity
Cowl, 22
Ice Chalet Cowl, 76–77
Kindling Stockings, 150–152
River Rock Throw, 124
Smokestack Ankle Socks, 60–61
Snowberry Hat, 66
Snowbird Blanket Shawl, 28
Snow Fern Cardigan, 34–36
Snow Tracks Headband, 72
Storm Flurry Wrap, 140
Winter Dreamer Pullover, 134–137
projects
Aspens Asymmetric Shawl, 108–121

Bräcken Frost Hat, 17–20
Campfire Stories Fingerless Mitts,
93–107
Campfire Stories Hat, 83–91
Cloud Cover Hood, 155–163
Cross Country Hooded Infinity
Cowl, 21–25
Ice Chalet Cowl, 74–79
Kindling Stockings, 149–154
River Rock Throw, 123–129
Smokestack Ankle Socks, 59–64
Snowberry Hat, 65–69
Snowbird Blanket Shawl, 27–31
Snow Fern Cardigan, 32–55
Snow Tracks Headband, 71–73
Storm Flurry Wrap, 139–147
Winter Dreamer Pullover, 133–138

R

River Rock Throw
chart instructions, 124–125
chart key, 126
chart (left), 129
chart (middle), 128
chart (right), 127
overview, 123–124
pattern, 124
schematic, 126

S

schematics
Aspens Asymmetric Shawl, 115
Bräcken Frost Hat, 19
Campfire Stories Fingerless Mitts,
99
Campfire Stories Hat, 87
Cloud Cover Hood, 160
Cross Country Hooded Infinity
Cowl, 25
Ice Chalet Cowl, 78
Kindling Stockings, 153
River Rock Throw, 126
Smokestack Ankle Socks, 63
Snowberry Hat, 68
Snowbird Blanket Shawl, 30
Snow Fern Cardigan, 37
Snow Tracks Headband, 72
Storm Flurry Wrap, 143
Winter Dreamer Pullover, 138
size: one size
Aspens Asymmetric Shawl, 108–121
Bräcken Frost Hat, 17–20
Campfire Stories Hat, 83–91

Cross Country Hooded Infinity
Cowl, 21–25
Ice Chalet Cowl, 74–79
River Rock Throw, 123–129
Snowberry Hat, 65–69
Snowbird Blanket Shawl, 27–31
size: one size, adult
Campfire Stories Fingerless Mitts,
93–107
Cloud Cover Hood, 155–163
Snow Tracks Headband, 71–73
Storm Flurry Wrap, 139–147
size: one size, teen: Cloud Cover
Hood, 155–163
size: 1–12
Snow Fern Cardigan, 32–55
Winter Dreamer Pullover, 133–138
size: 8–10
Kindling Stockings, 149–154
Smokestack Ankle Socks, 59–64
Smokestack Ankle Socks
chart instructions (left sock),
62–63
chart instructions (right sock), 62
chart key, 63
chart (left sock), 64
chart (right sock), 64
overview, 59–60
pattern, 60–61
schematic, 63
Snowberry Hat
chart, 69
chart instructions, 68
chart key, 69
overview, 65–66
pattern, 66
schematic, 68
Snowbird Blanket Shawl
chart A, 30
chart A instructions, 29
chart B, 31
chart B instructions, 29
chart key, 30
overview, 27
pattern, 28
schematic, 30
Snow Fern Cardigan
chart key, 38
chart (back, main body), 39
chart (back shoulder, size 1), 41
chart (back shoulder, size 2), 43
chart (back shoulder, size 3), 45
chart (back shoulder, size 4), 47
chart (back shoulder, size 5), 49

chart (back shoulder, size 6), 50
chart (back shoulder, size 7), 51
chart (back shoulder, size 8), 52
chart (back shoulder, size 9), 52
chart (back shoulder, size 10), 53
chart (back shoulder, size 11), 54
chart (back shoulder, size 12), 55
chart (left front, main body), 38
chart (left front shoulder, size 1), 40
chart (left front shoulder, size 2), 42
chart (left front shoulder, size 3), 44
chart (left front shoulder, size 4), 46
chart (left front shoulder, size 5), 48
chart (left front shoulder, size 6), 50
chart (left front shoulder, size 7), 51
chart (left front shoulder, size 8), 52
chart (left front shoulder, size 9), 52
chart (left front shoulder, size 10), 53
chart (left front shoulder, size 11), 54
chart (left front shoulder, size 12), 55
chart (right front, main body), 40
chart (right front shoulder, size 1), 42
chart (right front shoulder, size 2), 44
chart (right front shoulder, size 3), 46
chart (right front shoulder, size 4), 48
chart (right front shoulder, size 5), 48
chart (right front shoulder, size 6), 50
chart (right front shoulder, size 7), 51
chart (right front shoulder, size 8), 52
chart (right front shoulder, size 9), 52
chart (right front shoulder, size 10), 53
chart (right front shoulder, size 11), 54

chart (right front shoulder, size 12), 55
overview, 32–34
pattern, 34–36
schematic, 37
Snow Tracks Headband
chart, 73
chart instructions, 72
chart key, 72
overview, 71
pattern, 72
schematic, 72
Storm Flurry Wrap
chart (bottom left), 144
chart (bottom right), 145
chart instructions, 140–142
chart key, 143
chart (top left), 146
chart (top right), 147
overview, 139–140
pattern, 140
schematic, 143
super bulky weight yarn
Bräcken Frost Hat, 17–20
Cross Country Hooded Infinity
Cowl, 21–25
River Rock Throw, 123–129
Snowbird Blanket Shawl, 27–31

T
techniques
3-needle bind-off, 165
bobbles, 165
cable cast-on, 165
crochet chain, 165–166
crochet slip stitch, 166
German twisted longtail cast-on, 166
grafting, 24
I-cord, 167
Jeny's Surprisingly Stretchy Bind-off, 167
Judy's Magic cast-on, 167
Kitchener stitch, 168
longtail cast-on, 168
longtail tubular cast-on, 169
picking up and knitting stitches, 170
picot, 170
provisional cast-on, 170
sewn tubular bind-off, 170–171
shadow wrap knit (swk), 171
shadow wrap purl (swp), 171
triplet stitch (knit side), 171

triplet stitch (purl side), 171
twin stitch (knit side), 171
twin stitch (purl side), 171
tips and tricks
cable rows, 10
dropped stitches, 10–13
fiber selection, 8
left-leaning cable, 11, 12
locking stitch markers, 9, 10, 12
needle material, 8
needle selection, 9
practice projects, 9
reading your knitting, 10
right-leaning cable, 10–11
tools
cable needles, 8, 9
double-pointed needles, 9
fingers, 13
highlighters, 9
interchangeable tips, 9
locking stitch markers, 9, 10

W
Winter Dreamer Pullover
chart, 137
chart instructions, 137
chart key, 137
overview, 133–134
pattern, 134–137
schematic, 138
worsted weight yarn
Campfire Stories Fingerless Mitts, 93–107
Campfire Stories Hat, 83–91
Kindling Stockings, 149–154
Snowberry Hat, 65–69
Snow Tracks Headband, 71–73
Winter Dreamer Pullover, 133–138